Who's Afraid ...?

Who's Afraid ...?

Facing Children's Fears with Folktales

Norma J. Livo

Professor Emeritus
University of Colorado at Denver

1994
TEACHER IDEAS PRESS
A Division of
Libraries Unlimited, Inc.
Englewood, Colorado

For Helen Jackson O'Neil,
my beloved aunt,
who always made our four children
feel special and loved.

TEACHER IDEAS PRESS
A Division of
Libraries Unlimited, Inc.
P.O. Box 6633
Englewood, CO 80155-6633

1-800-237-6124

Library of Congress Cataloging-in-Publication Data

Livo, Norma J., 1929-
    Who's afraid ...? : facing children's fears with folktales / Norma
J. Livo.
    xxxii, 175 p. 17x25 cm.
    Includes bibliographical references and index.
    ISBN 0-87287-950-X
    1. Fear in children--Prevention. 2. Tales--Psychological aspects.
3. Children's stories. I. Title.
BF723.F4L58 1994   93-44319
155.4'1246--dc20   CIP

Contents

Acknowledgments

I acknowledge great help in the writing of this book. Thanks to my family, whose love, humor, and understanding gave me understanding of the importance of this book. George, my husband of more than 42 years, our four children—Lauren, Eric, Kim, and Robert—and their seven children have expanded my life experiences greatly.

Thanks also go to the folks of Libraries Unlimited, especially editors Suzanne Barchers and David Loertscher. I thank them all for their contributions to this book.

And to the researchers who studied children's fears, my special thanks go to Kaoru Yamamoto, Abdalla Soliman, James Parsons, and O. L. Davies Jr. for their fascinating insights.

Foreword

In fairy tales, a youth often sets out on a journey and along the way helps an ordinary animal—perhaps a horse, duck, lion, or even a bee. But, of course, the animal is not ordinary at all! It is, rather, a magical being—a fairy, an elf, even the king or queen of all the animals—and the creature later advises the youth in a terrible predicament. Norma Livo's latest book, *Who's Afraid . . .? Facing Children's Fears with Folktales*, reminds me of these magical creatures. Outwardly, the book may look like an ordinary teacher's text—a practical, pedagogical workhorse—offering ideas for classroom exercises and resources for further reading. But there is much more here, all of it magical. The book, in fact, is not only for teachers who work with children, but for all adults—for the "inner teacher" and the proverbial "inner child."

Livo begins with children's fears as enumerated by various researchers. For each anxiety, Livo provides several tales that show children and youths overcoming their fears. The stories, I might emphasize, do not reflect wishful thinking. There are no fairy godmothers to make problems vanish. The young protagonists succeed through wit, resourcefulness, courage, perseverance, and a little bit of luck—just like in real life.

While some of the children's anxieties may seem a little surprising at first, most adults will be able to empathize or recall similar apprehensions. Losing a parent, going blind, repeating a grade, and urinating in class are the top four for children. Yet these fears resurface in the adult years, particularly with midlife and old age. The fear of losing a parent becomes the fear of losing a child. Anxiety about going blind evolves into fear of cancer or heart attacks. Apprehension over repeating a grade changes into a fear of failing a promotion or having a marriage collapse. And the child's terror of urinating in public becomes the adult's anxiety over being unmasked as an impostor. The fears are human and timeless and so are the ways of coping with them, a fact that fairy tales depict clearly. Indeed, when frightened, we adults usually feel like children, and fairy tales offer advice and encouragement in these situations by using the ageless language of the unconscious. Fairy tales, in fact, link the generations: When parents tell stories to children, both learn from the telling and the parent's "inner child" emerges to listen, too.

Livo's selection of stories is remarkably broad, offering a tour through the world's many societies. As Livo rightly emphasizes, listening to stories helps us—children and adults alike—to empathize with other people. Through tales we discover our common human heritage behind "exotic" or "alien" customs. Such an ecumenical, multicultural spirit is sorely needed today as racial gangs do battle in American schools and "ethnic cleansing" ravages distant lands. The best place to start building this spirit of openness is surely with children and with that part of each adult that remembers the eager innocence of childhood.

For those who doubt that stories can have impact in the world, Livo provides poignant examples, drawing on her own experiences as a teacher, mother and grandmother, and from current events. A dramatic instance of the latter, at once chilling and inspiring, is that of Kassie Neou, who survived the atrocities of the Khmer Rouge death camps in Cambodia by telling stories. (I shall say no more, lest I spoil the impact of Livo's chapter!)

The tales in this anthology are important in another way: They present strong, resourceful girls in a positive light. There is no room here for helpless princesses who wait around for gallant princes to rescue them! By now, ample research demonstrates that many girls lose their self-confidence and give up their personal dreams in adolescence. Girls silence themselves in order to fit conventional standards of the "good girl" who does not argue, talk loudly, or make trouble. The courageous, outspoken girls in this book offer an alternative model. The stories function like a vaccination, conferring some degree of immunity against social pressures.

Ultimately, I think, that is the basic function of fairy tales and other folk stories. To help children—and adults—remain true to themselves on the long journey that is the human enterprise. The tales serve as maps and markers left by those who have successfully gone before. Livo's contribution is recognizing the signs and pointing them out to us—as teachers and children.

—Allan B. Chinen, M.D.
Author of *In the Ever After,*
Once Upon a Midlife, and
Beyond the Hero

Introduction

Where Stories Come From

(from the Seneca, the Huron, and the Wyandot)

There was a boy who hunted daily in the woods for food in another time long before this one. While on these trips he used to sit down beside a great rock to fix his bows or work on new arrow points. While sitting beside the rock one day he heard a voice: "Let me tell you a story."

The boy looked carefully around him and then circled the rock looking for the owner of the voice. He decided that it must be a magic rock that had the ability to talk. Even though he was afraid, he asked the rock, "What story do you want to tell me?"

"Before I start, you must give me a gift. Then I will tell you an ancient story that will explain many things to you," said the voice.

"This morning I killed this pheasant. Will this do as a present?" asked the boy as he carefully placed the bird on top of the boulder.

"Yes, it will do nicely. Come back in the twilight, and I will tell you about another time and the way of the world during that time," came the answer from the stone.

Just as the sun was ready to set below the far distant hillside, the boy returned to the rock. He settled down on the moss beside the stone, and the voice began:

"Since there was no Earth, the first people lived beyond the sky. The people had a great chief, and he had a beautiful daughter whom he loved dearly. She became sick, and nothing could be found to cure her.

"The great chief consulted the wise old man who knew many things. He told the chief to dig up a large tree and lay the sick girl beside the hole. The chief ordered his son to dig up an especially fine tree. Because there were many strong young men and they cared deeply for both their chief and his daughter, they dug a huge hole. Suddenly, before they could lift the tree out, the tree fell right down through the bottom of the hole. Worst of all, the girl fell along with it.

"Below there was a vast sea of water that had two swans floating on it. The swans became alarmed at a sudden thunderclap and looked up. Just as they did, they saw the sky fall apart, and they watched the huge tree fall into the water. The waves made by the gigantic tree hadn't calmed down before the swans saw a girl also falling from the sky. The swans could see that she was quite beautiful and didn't want her to drown or get hurt, so they swam to her to support her. They knew they needed help, though, so they swam to the Great Turtle who was the master of all the animals. The Great Turtle called a council of all the animals immediately. Great Turtle announced to all the assembled animals that this beautiful girl falling from the sky was a sign of future good fortune. He explained that they needed to find where the tree had sunk because it had earth entwined in its roots. He told them to bring back some of the earth to put on his back and make an island for the girl to live on.

"One of the animals asked the Great Turtle how they would know where to look, and the answer was that the swans would lead them because they had seen where the tree had fallen.

"The swans did indeed remember where the tree had splashed into the water. Three of the animals were chosen to dive for the earth. First Otter, then Muskrat, and then Beaver. One after the other each dived to the depths, and one after the other when each animal came back from the dive, it rolled over so exhausted that it died. After them, many other animals tried to bring up some earth, but each met the same fate. The last animal to volunteer was the old lady Toad. She made the dive and was below for a long time. All of the animals thought that she too was lost.

"At last she surfaced with a splash and a gasp and spit a mouthful of earth onto the back of the Great Turtle. Then she gave another gasp and died.

"The earth old lady Toad had brought up was magical and started to grow. It grew until it was as big as an island, and then the maiden was set down on it by the two white swans. They continued to swim around the island, and it grew and grew until it became the world island we know today."

When the voice finished, it told the boy that his eyelids were drooping and his head was nodding and that he was about to fall asleep. "It will be better if you come back tomorrow evening, and I will tell you more of the story. Remember to bring my present," said the boulder.

The next evening as dusk was falling the boy returned to the rock with a string of rabbits. He put them carefully on top of the stone and sat down to hear the next story.

The voice began: "This new world, wonderful as it was, had a big problem. It was dark. Everywhere it was dark. There was no light anywhere. Great Turtle called all the animals together again to find a solution to the darkness. They decided to put a great light high in the sky. The next problem was that there was no one who could do this. Great Turtle turned to Little Turtle and asked her if she could do this great task. Little Turtle thought and then shyly offered that she might be able to climb the dangerous unknown path to the sky. Everyone invoked their own magical powers to help Little Turtle. Their magic formed a great black cloud that was full of clashing rocks that made lightning whenever they smashed together.

"Brave Little Turtle climbed into this cloud and was carried around the sky. She collected all the lightning she could find as she went. She made a big bright ball out of it, and then she threw this ball as far as she could into the sky. She looked at it all and decided that more light was needed, so she gathered more lightning for a smaller ball. She again threw it as far into the sky as she could. The first big ball became the sun, and the second smaller ball became the moon.

"Great Turtle studied the sky and then ordered the burrowing animals to make holes in the corners of the sky so that the sun and moon could go down through one and climb up again through the other as they circled the sky. Great Turtle bent his neck to look at the sky and smiled. Now there was day and night."

The boy returned to the rock each evening with a gift and heard more stories. His friend became curious about where he went each night. The boy told him that he went to listen to stories. The friend wondered what stories were, but the boy couldn't explain them. So he told his friend to go with him that night to find out for himself. As the sun glowed red over the horizon, the boy and his friend placed gifts on top of the storytelling stone. They heard more amazing stories and then went home to their beds.

The news of the stone and the stories swept through the village, and the boys were asked to lead their people to the place where the stone rested in the Earth. The people took the meat of deer with them that they left respectfully on the top of the rock. They all marveled over the stories they heard that night. They learned things that even the wisest among them had never known. And so the stone continued to tell the stories for four years. Then, all the tales had been told.

That last evening after all the others had gone, the boulder told the boy to stay. "When you are old and not able to hunt, tell these stories to others. But make sure that the people give you something in return for them," said the stone. After the voice of the rock had told the boy this it became silent and never spoke again.

And so it was that as an old man he told the stories to everyone who would come to him to listen. Listeners gladly gave him tobacco, furs, meat, and feathers. This is the way stories came to be and why there are many stories in the world today. The people from the world before ours gave us the strong, wonderful stories we tell one another even today.

Using Stories

The term using stories does not imply that when you "use" stories they are all used up and gone. Far from it. Stories are like the Energizer bunny: They just go on giving. This book uses stories as reference and discussion points for the topics of children's fears.

What is a story? It depends on who hears it. As listeners and readers we all discover different things in the same story. Some things we are ready for, and some stories we just skim the top off. The same story can leave one person with a smile and another with tears. Whether we know it or not, we are all guided by voices of our ancestors—they had generations of memory in their heads. More about the ancient stories and oral history later.

Stories of events and peoples (animals) that are real, remembered, historical, or embellished are all part of us. There is none among us who is too old or too sophisticated to be touched by a story. As proof of this, consider the case of Kassie S. Neou of the Cambodian Survivors Association who was held prisoner by the Khmer Rouge, the Cambodian Communist party. At an address at the Denver Museum of Natural History he remembered: "I was taken to jail in 1976 because I spoke three words of English. That was my crime. I survived execution just because guards wanted to keep me alive to tell them stories—Aesop stories."

The Japanese believe that people are not dead until people stop saying their names. Is that why families have unconsciously or consciously named their children after other family members? We have David John Jackson, Sr., David John Jackson, Jr., and David John Jackson, III, in our family as well as variations on the name *Lavina*. Names and stories give us immortality.

What are some of the other values of stories? Some say that stories make us more human. They help us live more lives than we have. Stories help us see the world from inside the skins of people different from ourselves. They help develop compassion and insight into the behavior of ourselves and others. A good story can show us the past in a way that helps us understand the present. One of the most important features of a story is that it develops the imagination. Stories also help us entertain ideas we never could have had without them. Stories are magical: They can take us out of ourselves and return us to ourselves a changed self-transforming power.

Stories can be used to build self-confidence and persistence, to impart values and hopes, to demonstrate follies and triumphs, and to develop an optimistic outlook on life and show the listener or the reader that he or she is not the only one who ever experienced problems. There is no such thing as a story being only a story.

Ancient stories are the best stories because they have been worked on over the ages by the "folk." Folk stories, or fairy tales, are simply essential to the development of children. The seemingly simple folk story is a combination of entertainment, history, astronomy, religion, literature, and social and natural science. The eminent child psychologist Bruno Bettelheim felt that folk stories teach children that they have to meet danger, or do battle, and that only in this way will they grow up.

There have always been people who would avoid these stories or sanitize them. According to Bettelheim, Charles Dickens expressed scorn for those wishing to ban fairy tales because, "Dickens understood that the imagery of fairy tales helps children better than anything else in their most difficult and yet most important and satisfying task: achieving a more mature consciousness to civilize the chaotic pressures of their unconscious."[1] Bettelheim went on to say:

> Each fairy tale is a magic mirror which reflects some aspects of our inner world, and of the steps required by our evolution from immaturity to maturity. For those who immerse themselves in what the fairy tale has to communicate, it becomes a deep, quiet pool which at first seems to reflect only our own image; but behind it we soon discover the inner turmoils of our soul—its depth, and ways to gain peace within ourselves and with the world, which is the reward of our struggles.[2]

The ability to tell stories—by the ancient peoples as well as today's suburbanites—is the only art that exists in all human cultures. It is through stories that we experience our lives. The ability to story is what sets people apart from all the other creatures of the Earth. It may be the one element that defines us as humans.

With the advent of print, stories are now frozen in books. We no longer spend the long, dark winter nights telling one another stories. In fact, one opponent of too much television in our lives said that the light bulb—not television—destroyed storytelling. However it goes, we now learn most of our stories from books. For the purposes of this book, this is not bad. At least it gives us access to the stories that can help children cope with their fears. A great story is something that one cannot step into twice at the same place—somewhat like Heraclitus's river from mythology. That is the reason for the use of stories in relation to helping children vanquish fears. Children find in stories something to build on for future experiences—different spots in the river.

Why Are Animals So Important as Characters in Stories?

It is not because animals are so darn cute. There is much more to it than that. Maybe it is because animals are just a bit different from real children and people that the dramatic events of a folktale are a little easier to handle. Animals help us follow the story with a little bit of distance to it, that is, they impart enough psychological distance to keep a frightening story from being truly terrifying. Sometimes we need the disguise or symbolism of animals to talk about what is important. Animals are neuter. They aren't specific like Aunt Marge (crazy Aunt Marge) or Uncle Elmer (cruel Uncle Elmer). Animals can be ourselves in fur, feather, or fin, but as characters they make the story medicine a little easier to take. Stories are rehearsals for the future, and as such animals make this easier.

Animals can also be symbols: the sly fox, the clever wolf, or the powerful bear. Sometimes it is helpful for children to see a helpless animal such as a rabbit outsmart an animal that is big and strong. After all, aren't children pretty helpless in the world of adults? Wouldn't it be easy for them to unconsciously relate to Br'er Rabbit as he outwits the other animals? Can't that give children a sense of power, an "I can do it too" spirit?

What Stories Do

People have used stories such as the tale of where stories came from to explain how things should be, the way to behave properly, how things came to be, as well as the creation of our world. The layers of meanings in a story fit the level of understanding of each particular listener and reader. We can go back to the same story and discover much more in it at different stages of our lives.

In the story "Where Stories Come From," we might look at some of the possible symbolism in it. It is important to know that Native Americans believe everything has life. Everything. With this thought, it is easy to see how the rock could represent the Earth or the world. The gifts could be symbols of the work we do in the world—our treasures, the very best that we can leave behind when we are gone.

Let's look at another story and examine some of its messages. In *Seven Arrows*, Hyemeyohsts Storm tells the story of Jumping Mouse.[3] It follows in an abbreviated form.

Once there was a mouse, a busy curious mouse. He heard, however, a roaring in his ears that the other mice did not hear. Finally he decided to investigate the noise. He met a raccoon who explained to him that the roaring he heard was the river. Because the mouse did not know what a river was, the raccoon took him to see it. Even though the mouse was filled with fear, he went with his heart pounding. He smelled things he had never smelled before as they walked on strange paths.

The river was breathtaking and powerful. At the river, raccoon introduced mouse to a frog. The frog told mouse about the magic of the river and then had him jump as high into the air as he was able. When mouse did this, he saw the sacred mountains that were far off. Frog named him Jumping Mouse after this.

Jumping Mouse returned to the world of the mice, but no one believed him or could understand his vision. The memory, though, burned in Jumping Mouse's heart. He returned to the river and the prairie. He looked up and saw eagles. He was determined to travel to the sacred mountains. Gathering all his courage he ran to some sage. There he met an old mouse. The old mouse tried to discourage Jumping Mouse from his quest. The old mouse wanted Jumping Mouse to stay with him where they had everything they needed for a good life. Jumping Mouse, though, gathered his determination and started on his journey again. He met a buffalo who was sick and dying. Buffalo told Jumping Mouse that only the eye of a mouse would heal him.

Jumping Mouse did not want such a great being to die, so he offered the buffalo one of his eyes. The eye flew out of his head, and the buffalo was saved. Buffalo encouraged Jumping Mouse to continue his quest, and so they traveled to the foot of the sacred mountains with the mouse scurrying in the shadow of the buffalo to protect himself from the eagles.

In this new place Jumping Mouse found an abundance of seeds and other things. He met a gray wolf who was having trouble with his memory. Jumping Mouse knew that his eye would cure the wolf, so he offered it to him. The eye flew out of Jumping Mouse's head, and the wolf was made whole. The wolf became the blind mouse's guide into the sacred mountains. He guided him through the pines to a lake with the world reflected in it, and then he left Jumping Mouse. Jumping Mouse heard a sound that eagles make and felt a shadow on his back. The eagle hit and Jumping Mouse fell asleep.

When Jumping Mouse woke up he was surprised that he was still alive, but, amazingly, he could see again. A blurry shape came toward him, and a voice told him to jump as high as he could. Jumping Mouse did as he was told. Then he heard the voice telling him to hang on to the wind and trust and not be afraid. Jumping Mouse did and found himself being carried higher and higher. He flew over his old friend the frog who called to him: "You have a new name. You are Eagle."

This story is an example of a personal and cultural myth. When we hear the great roar, are we willing to take risks with great physical and emotional sacrifices? Can we abandon security and the known in the quest for the unknown? Can we climb the mountain and become changed?

The archetypes in this story are many. This is the ancient call to the quest, and it is about a compulsion to reach a higher plain. It is the metaphor of an individual who becomes assertive and overcomes the pressure to conform. Jumping Mouse overcomes his fears and transcends them. There are helpers who guide him on his journey, but it is Jumping Mouse who gives freely and attains his new life when he faces death. Obviously he becomes spiritually strong and wise. Instead of being a little mouse who is content to see only what is right before him as he searches a limited space and busily looks for food, he is curious and dares to travel to new places, to look higher than just at ground level, and to trust creatures that could easily end his life. He makes sacrifices that help him to see things in a new way even in his blindness. To Jumping Mouse, all the creatures he meets are monsters. He overcomes his fear of these giants. He has metaphorically made the leap of faith, persisted, and overcome.

In many world mythologies there are stories of giving eyes to others. In the Egyptian myth the god Horus lost an eye and gave it to the dead Osiris to eat. Osiris was then equipped with a soul. There is an African folk story about a jaguar who plays endless games of having his eyes fly away until he calls them back. They accidentally become eaten by a fish. A vulture makes the jaguar some new eyes, but he exacts a promise that whatever beast the jaguar kills while out hunting, he must always leave a piece for the vulture. Folklorists theorize that the tearing out of the eye appears to be connected with the creation or re-creation of the sun or the moon. There are many echoes in primitive stories of sunrise and sunset connected with the sacrifice of eyes.

And so there are many possible meanings in the story of Jumping Mouse. Many of these messages are obvious; others are imbedded in the unconscious and evoked by archetypes of ancient times.

Everyday stories by everyday people can also develop connections for us. One of my former students told that as she brushed the tangles out of her daughter's hair there were constant complaints and whining. Then the mother started to tell her daughter stories about herself as a child and what she thought and felt as her mother brushed her hair. The whining and complaining stopped, and the little girl began to ask for another "mommy story" every time the hairbrushing ritual began.

In Defense of Monsters and Dangers in Stories

Children experience monsters and dangers on their own. We cannot keep these threats away from them. They invent many more amazing monsters themselves than we could think of. Let me relate a personal experience about one of our children and a monster. Our son was four years old. We lived in an old house on a hillside with several acres of trees alongside. One day our son, Mike, came screaming in terror into the house, ran up the stairs to his bedroom, and threw himself—still screaming—under his bed. I followed him up as fast as I could to see what the terror was all about. I had to physically drag him out from under the bed and restrain him in my arms as I tried to question him. He finally calmed down enough to tell me that there was a giant with a sharp, huge ax out in the woods. He said the giant had threatened to kill him. Hoping that too much time had not intervened, I carried Mike out of his room, down the stairs, and out of the house. He reverted to hysterics when he saw I intended to take him into those very woods. I called as calmly as I could to whomever was there to please come and help me. I said my son was terrified and that I meant no harm. I only wanted my son to see them and talk with them. I heard some noises among the bushes and headed in that direction repeating my request. Finally an eight-year-old came out from behind a tree very cautiously. I kept assuring him I only wanted to help my son see that he was not a giant. Mike buried his face in my shoulder and would not look at the boy I was talking to for quite some time. When he finally did look, he was amazed. This was no giant, just an older boy. Then my son asked to see the sharp, shiny hatchet. The boy brought out the dullest little knife from his belt holder that I had ever seen. I asked him if my son could hold it in his hands to examine it. Well, of course, before it was all over, Mike was able to stand on his own feet and to talk with the former giant by himself.

After this we told our son a lot of giant stories with young boys who took care of such dramatic dangers themselves. These stories, including "Jack and the Beanstalk" and "David and Goliath," helped him to see that other seemingly helpless, small characters were able to conquer their fears and persevere in their battles and win. (Today he still slays giants in the real world of adults.)

A bogey is an imaginary evil being or spirit or goblin—anything that one especially, and often needlessly, fears. A bogeyman is an imaginary and frightful being, especially one used as a threat to children in disciplining them. Bogeymen threats to children are universal in folk stories.

There are many frightful beings worldwide with different names and stories concerning them. Think of the stories about dragons, Bigfoot, the yeti, the Loch Ness Monster, Norggens (large, malevolent giants known to eat children), the Armenian Nhang (a monstrous evil spirit that sometimes appears in rivers as a woman or as a seal that drags swimmers to the bottom), the South German Berchta, and Baba Yaga (the Russian folklore cannibalistic ogress who steals and cooks her victims—preferably children).

In the American Southwest the most famous of these frightful beings is La Llorona, or the "weeping woman." Around her has arisen a story I have heard from dozens of people. There are many variations on this story and quite a bit of speculation as to its origins. In 1977 the cartoonist Gus Arriola devoted 29 daily *Gordo* cartoons to some of the beliefs around La Llorona.[4] People living today in the San Luis Valley of Colorado and New Mexico swear the story is real and is set there. As a living part of the oral tradition, there are those who say it originated in Oaxaca in southern Mexico. It has also been traced to the Aztecs. There are hundreds of versions of La Llorona, and they can be found in Central America, South America, and Spain. Clearly she is a standard apparition wherever the heritage of Spanish legendry exists. She is probably the most famous and most believed character in apparitional history.[5]

Who is La Llorona? I first heard about her from a wide-eyed third-grader, and the skeleton of the story as she told it to me is quite simple. A young woman married to an older man wanted to dance and have fun, but instead she had to stay at home to tend her children and husband. One night in a fit of petulance she decided that to enjoy life she must run away from her husband. She drowned her children in a stream. That is why children who are out at night or who have been naughty hear wailing and moaning and screaming along waterways or at wells. It is La Llorona, who was sentenced to search throughout eternity for her children, and she takes away any children she can find.

The details of the story vary with the tellers, and usually—even today—tellers swear that they know exactly where it happened and that the story is true. I have talked with people who tell me firsthand stories of this ghost.

Basically, though, La Llorona has been characterized either as a kidnapper of infants (in retribution for the child she lost in its infancy) or as a mourner of dead infants. She is also viewed as a threat to infants or as a solace for grieving parents—depending on the tale itself. The father generally is nonexistent or immaterial to the story.

All these folk versions of the story have several levels of meaning. Parents tell me they now use the story themselves with their own children to emphasize the dangers of being out after dark, playing near the water, and not obeying their parents. These are always the conditions present when La Llorona is searching for her children or other children to take their place. Other levels of meaning felt by people who tell the story are that it warns adults to cherish their children, to be faithful, and to avoid pre- and extramarital sex, and they predict the punishment if this advice is not heeded. I have gathered this information over the years by interviewing people who tell La Llorona stories. The story has lasted until the present because its original folk message was so strong. That message has been adapted for the places the story has traveled and has assumed details to fit the new location. Its influence has been felt through the ages and continues to be passed on today.

The following letter from Tom Weakley came to me as a result of an article, "Bogeyman (or Woman) Stories," printed in the National Association for the Preservation and Perpetuation of Storytelling news publication *Yarnspinner*.[6] Tom worked in Nigeria in the summer of 1991 as part of the Earth Watch project to find water to fill the canals which used to get water from Lake Chad and help the people in the drought-stricken country. His letter is so special and eloquent in its message about the importance of stories for children worldwide that we include it here.

Another bogeyman story is the Ute's "Basket Woman." The Ute once occupied most of present-day Colorado, eastern Utah, and northern New Mexico. They were loosely organized into seven bands: the Tabequash, Yampa, Mouache, Unita, Capote, Weeminuchi, and the Uncompaghre.

I first heard about Basket Woman in October 1987. A group of us called Storytellers on Tour were traveling throughout Colorado telling stories, conducting workshops, and participating in concerts in towns that arranged for our visits through the Colorado Council for the Arts and Humanities. This particular day we were in Cortez doing an afternoon session. The five of us told stories for the folks who came to hear us, and I observed a group of Ute folks in the audience. During our break, I asked them if they would share some of their stories when we reconvened. They consulted with one another, and then four of them pointed to another. "Betty, you tell the story of Basket Woman best," they said. "You do it."

So when we gathered again, Betty introduced us to Basket Woman, and it is Betty's story that follows.

Cackling old Basket Woman was creeping up on children who were still out after they should have been home. She was a huge ogress and carried a basket on her back which was made of woven snakes.

She found a child and whacked it on its head with her cane and threw the child into her basket. She found a second one and thunked it and tossed it on top of the other child. The third child was harder to catch, but she finally caught him, clobbered him on his head, and flung him into the basket with the other two children. She really had to sneak up on the fourth child. She whacked him on his head and flipped him into her basket. Then she took off—cackling loudly—for her home up on Ute Mountain.

She had put on a pot of water to boil before she left to catch the children for her supper, and it was boiling and bubbling nicely. She liked to eat tender children and was licking her lips in anticipation.

(Story continues on page xxvi.)

TOM WEAKLEY   RD 1 Box 1160   Arlington, VT 05250   (802) 375-6934

August 19, 1993

Norma J. Livo
c/o Yarnspinner
NAPPS
P.O. Box 309
Jonesborough, TN 37659

Dear Norma Livo:

I have just read your article on Bogeymen in the new Yarnspinner, and I wanted
to confirm your thesis that La Llorona*is a universal character--or someone
very much like her is.

I was in northern Nigeria a couple of summers ago working as a volunteer on a
project to help locate new sources of water for this drought-stricken area.
I noted that many of the village wells were simple holes in the sand--no
wall, no overhanging support--just a hole maybe 50 yards out from the edge of
the village. I asked the Nigerian engineer who accompanied us to the villages
about this. "How do you keep children from playing out here? Aren't the
villagers afraid the children might slip and fall into the well?" (Some of
these wells went down 100 feet.)

"No," he answered, "the children never play out here."

Well, there were kids everywhere I looked. They were milling around us as we
worked to draw water from the wells to test it. "Do you tell them stories
about someone who to frighten them away from this place?"

"No, we have no stories about wells."

"Maybe a story about someone who will 'get them' if they go too close to the
wells?"

"No, we have no stories like that," he said.

"In parts of my country," I told him, "parents will tell their children not to
go near the river or wander down to the lake or the canals because there is a
person down there, usually a woman, who lives in the water and who cries out
for her lost child. And if they get too close to the water or the canal, she
will reach out her hand and grab their leg and drag them into the water."

The engineer turned toward me. "Oh! You mean Mommy Water?"

Somehow, he did not think of 'Mommy Water' as a story, it was so much a part
of village life and lore. But there she was--in this remote settlement of
grass and mud huts under the sub-Saharan sun. Old La Llorona herself.

I enjoyed your article a lot. Thanks.

Tom Weakley

* I had not heard of this name until I read your article.

What Basket Woman didn't know was that the father of one of the missing children discovered his child was gone and started out looking for him. He saw Basket Woman as she was sneaking up on the fourth child, so he followed her. Following her wasn't hard since she cackled so much on her way up to Ute Mountain and could be heard all through the forest.

Just as Basket Woman was getting ready to put the children into the boiling pot, the father took off his beaded headband and swung it out at her. When it hit her she fell into the bubbling hot water and started to shrivel. She melted and disappeared completely.

The children all came back to life and ran home. They always made sure they got home before it was dark after that.

Since I first heard this story I have also collected variants of it from Samish people of the Northwest. These versions are more elaborate and contain chants and songs. And in them it is either a hunchback boy who saves the others, or he runs home and gets help to save the children. The basket that the ogress carries is either a burden basket or a clam basket. Vi Hilbert includes four versions of Basket Woman in her book *Haboo*.[7]

An Acoma version I heard in Santa Fe in 1988 tells of the time many giants and monsters still lived near the village and roamed about carrying huge baskets on their backs. They too caught people to eat. One man who had stayed too long hunting found out that his wife has disappeared. He found her with others in the home of one of the giants near the highest peak in the Zuni Mountains. The husband called to the giant who caught him and as she was washing him to cook, he convinced her to look out of her window for a cooling breeze. When she did, he jumped over to the fire and threw one of the hot stones from the fireplace at her. She fell out of the window and down a cliff, where she died. He then freed everyone, and they all left for their homes.

In either telling Basket Woman is clearly another effective bogeyman who helps keep children aware that they should be home when they are supposed to be and who helps adults recognize how they should behave. I know these two folklore characters are effective because I have been told by many Hispanics that they heard about La Llorona as children and that the story made them pay attention to their families' warnings about watching out when they were near water and being home before dark. The same is true for the Ute women who told us their story. They all remembered it as an important threat when they were children and as a form of disciplining them.

With what is happening in our society today with the kidnapping and molesting of young children, maybe we need to help La Llorona and Basket Woman out and invent new bogeymen to serve as warnings to our young people. Some older European stories that told children of certain dangers—"Little Red Riding Hood," for example, with its warning to little girls—have been rewritten so many times and sanitized that their serious messages have been lost in cuteness. That is certainly not true with Basket Woman and La Llorona. These stories are still part of the oral tradition and have only recently been recorded in print. Maybe these stronger bogeymen could be used more widely. At least, they seem to be functioning quite well in the West.

Many a timid child has been terrorized by an intimidating adult who says, "I could eat you up" as they pinch the child's cheeks. We have seen this child-eating idea in "Hansel and Gretel" and the "Basket Woman." But a look at children-eating monsters would not be complete without Baba Yaga. As mentioned earlier, she is a cannibalistic ogress who steals and cooks her victims and who lives in a hut that constantly spins around on fowls' legs in a clearing in the forest. The hut is surrounded by a picket fence topped with skulls. Baba Yaga rides through the air in an iron kettle or in a mortar that she moves by a pestle as she sweeps her traces from the air with a broom.

Yes, the messages of these folklore characters are scary and cruel, but there seems to have been a place for bogeymen throughout the ages. Children can learn to cope with dangers through these stories.

Activities

- Read or tell these stories in this book. Share them with children.

- Discuss the stories. What are the messages in the story? Children will amaze you with their perceptions of what they find in the story.

- After sharing the story, extend the experience with an art project. For instance, have the children draw pictures of what they saw. This will help children see, externalize, and face their fears.

- Have children tell an ending to a monster story that changes it into a pleasant experience or gives them control over the monster.

- If you are working with children in the classroom, have the children develop the story into a readers' theater script and perform it for another group.

- Suggest that the listener and the reader compare and contrast the story with another one they remember.

- Have the child write an original story.

- In considering giants, ask the children to check out books on Jack and the beanstalk. There are many in print. Then have the children compare and contrast these books. They could make a chart to keep their observations organized.

Bibliography

Arnold, Caroline. *The Terrible Hodag.* Illustrations by Lambert Davis. San
    Diego, Calif.: Harcourt Brace Jovanovich, 1989.
    Tales of the Hodag have been told around campfires in the northern
woods for more than 100 years. A logger named Ole Swenson befriends the
terrible Hodag, who helps him run the boss man out of the forest.

Chase, Richard. *The Jack Tales.* Boston: Houghton Mifflin, 1943.
    Folktales from the Southern Appalachians are collected and retold by
Chase.

Cole, Joanna. "The Baba Yaga." In *Best Loved Folk-Tales*, 411-14. Garden
    City, N.Y.: The Anchor Press/Doubleday, 1982.
    A stepmother sends her stepdaughter to Baba Yaga, but the girl is no
fool and outsmarts them.

De Regniers, Beatrice Schenk. *Jack and the Beanstalk.* Illustrations by Anne
    Wilsdorf. New York: Aladdin Books, 1985.
    Retelling in verse of the old tale of Jack, the bean stalk, and the giant.

____. *Jack the Giant-Killer.* Illustrations by Anne Wilsdorf. New York:
    Atheneum, 1987.
    Retells Jack's encounter with a giant, including such lore as the right
way to shake hands with a giant.

Faulkner, Matt. *Jack and the Beanstalk.* New York: Scholastic, 1986.
    The classic tale of clever Jack, who climbs a bean stalk and outwits a
hungry giant.

Fisher, Leonard Everett. *Cyclops.* New York: Holiday House, 1991.
    Describes the encounter between the Cyclops Polyphemus and Odys-
seus and his men after the end of the Trojan War.

Fukami, Haruo. *An Orange for a Bellybutton.* Minneapolis, Minn.: Carol-
    rhoda, 1990.
    A giant takes an orange for a belly button, but trouble for both ensues
before they are able to accept the right life for each.

Gackenbach, Dick. *Harry and the Terrible Whatzit.* Boston: Houghton Mifflin,
    1977.
    When his mother goes to the cellar and does not return right away,
Harry goes down to search for her and confronts the terrible two-headed
Whatzit.

Garner, Alan. *Jack and the Beanstalk*. Illustrations by Julek Heller. New York: Doubleday, 1992.
A boy climbs to the top of a giant bean stalk, where he uses his quick wits to outsmart an ogre and make his and his mother's fortune.

Haley, Gail E. *Go Away, Stay Away*. New York: Charles Scribner's Sons, 1977.
The village people join in a festival to free themselves of the demons, goblins, and spirits that cause their misfortunes. This is based on one of the spring festivals held in many parts of the world to drive out any evil spirits that may be lurking after the winter. The people dress up in masks and costumes in order to frighten off their unwelcomed visitors.

____. *Jack and the Beantree*. New York: Crown, 1986.
The classic story of Jack outwitting the giant.

____. *Jack and the Fire Dragon*. New York: Crown, 1988.
Jack encounters the menacing monster known as the Dragman and rescues three beautiful sisters from the monster's underground cave.

____. *Mountain Jack Tales*. New York: Dutton, 1992.
The hero of these stories is Jack, and the stories are set in the mountains of North Carolina but have their roots in old-world folklore.

Hayes, Joe. *La Llorona the Weeping Woman*. El Paso, Tex.: Cinco Puntos Press, 1987.

Hoban, Russell. *Monsters*. Illustrations by Quentin Blake. New York: Scholastic, 1989.
John's obsession with drawing monsters takes him to a doctor, and a startling discovery is made about the degree of reality of John's drawings.

Hutchins, Pat. *The Very Worst Monster*. New York: Greenwillow, 1985.
Hazel sets out to prove that she, not her baby brother, is the worst monster anywhere.

Kellogg, Steven. *Jack and the Beanstalk*. New York: Morrow Junior Books, 1991.
The classic story of Jack, the bean stalk, and the giant.

Kimmel, Eric A. *Baba Yaga, a Russian Folktale*. Illustrations by Megan Lloyd. New York: Holiday House, 1991.
When a terrible witch vows to eat her for supper, a little girl escapes with the help of a towel and comb given to her by the witch's cat.

King, Larry L. *Because of Lozo Brown.* Illustrations by Amy Schwartz. New
York: Viking Kestrel, 1988.
A little boy is afraid to meet his new neighbor, Lozo Brown, until they
begin to play and become friends.

McGilvray, Richard. *Don't Climb Out of the Window Tonight.* Illustrations by
Alan Snow. New York: Dial, 1993.
Flying ghosts and jogging giants are just two of the ten very good
reasons a little girl makes up so she won't climb out of her window in the
middle of the night. Written by a seven-year-old child.

Morton, Miriam. *A Harvest of Russian Children's Literature.* Berkeley, Calif.:
University of California Press, 1967.
A collection of monster stories, including the story of Baba Yaga and
dragons.

Mueller, Virginia. *Monster and the Baby.* Illustrations by Lynn Munsinger.
New York: Puffin Books, 1985.
Trying to entertain his baby brother by building a tower out of blocks,
Monster finds there is only one way to stop him from crying.

Prelutsky, Jack. *Something Big Has Been Here.* Illustrations by James Steven-
son. New York: Greenwillow, 1990.
A witty, funny anthology of poems, including some to raise the little
hairs on the back of the neck.

Rael, Elsa Okon. *Marushka's Egg.* Illustrations by Joanna Wezyk. New York:
Four Winds Press, 1993.
Nine-year-old Marushka is sucked into a magic egg, where she is
forced to be housekeeper to the witch Baba Yaga.

Ratnett, Michael. *Peter and the Bogeyman.* Illustrations by June Goulding.
New York: Barron's, 1989.
Warned that the bogeyman will turn him into salt if he is naughty,
Peter sets out to catch the bogeyman and turn him into salt.

Ross, Tony. *Happy Blanket.* New York: Farrar, Straus and Giroux, 1990.
Gregory and Lucy know that the scary things in life are not as threatening with a "happy blanket" around for protection. The stories of Gregory
and Lucy begin at either end of the book and meet in the middle for an
unusual glimpse into the real world of a child's imagination.

San Souci, Robert D. *Thirty Chilling Tales Short and Shivery.* Illustrations by
    Katherine Coville. New York: Doubleday, 1989.
    A collection of 30 short and spooky tales from the folklore of Russia,
Virginia, Ireland, Canada, and other areas of the world.

Small, Ernest, and Blair Lent. *Baba Yaga.* Boston: Houghton Mifflin, 1966.
    (Ernest Small is a pseudonym for Blair Lent.)
    The author has drawn together much of the Baba Yaga lore of Russian
folktales.

Steptoe, John. *The Story of Jumping Mouse.* New York: Lothrop, Lee &
    Shepard, 1984.
    This is a retold story of a Native American legend.

Ungerer, Tomi. *Zeralda's Ogre.* New York: Delacorte, 1967.
    The giant appetite of the ogre could only be satisfied by the flesh of
children until young Zeralda tamed his taste buds with her culinary art.

Waddell, Martin, and Penny Dale. *Once There Were Giants.* New York:
    Delacorte, 1989.
    As a baby girl grows up and becomes an adult, the "giants" in her
family seem to grow smaller.

Whitlock, Susan Love. *Donovan Scares the Monsters.* Illustrations by Yossi
    Abolafia. New York: Greenwillow, 1987.
    While visiting his grandparents, Donovan searches their house for
monsters, which he scares away with his grandparents' help.

Williams, Marcia. *Not a Worry in the World.* New York: Crown, 1990.
    A boy learns how to chase away the ever-escalating fears that plague
him.

Winthrop, Elizabeth. *Maggie and the Monster.* Illustrations by Tomie
    dePaola. New York: Holiday House, 1987.
    Maggie wants to get rid of the monster that visits her room every night
and accepts her mother's suggestion to simply ask the monster what it
wants.

_____. *Vasilissa the Beautiful: A Russian Folktale.* Illustrations by Alexander
    Koshkin. New York: HarperCollins, 1991.
    A beautifully illustrated retelling of a Russian fairy tale about the
beautiful Vasilissa and her struggles with her wicked stepmother and
stepsisters. Vasilissa uses her magic doll to escape from the witch Baba
Yaga.

References

Bettelheim, Bruno. *The Uses of Enchantment: The Meaning and Importance of Fairy Tales*. New York: Knopf, 1976.
    Bettelheim develops his theory about why fairy tales are so important in the emotional and social development of children.

Hilbert, Vi, ed. and trans. *Haboo*. Seattle: University of Washington Press, 1985.
    Hilbert has given us a collection of and explanation for Native American stories from the Puget Sound.

Kraul, Edward Garcia, and Judith Beatty. *The Weeping Woman: Encounters with La Llorona*. Santa Fe, N.Mex.: The Word Process, 1988.
    The authors give us a discussion of La Llorona along with many variants of the story.

Livo, Norma J., and Sandra A. Rietz. *Storytelling: Process and Practice*. Littleton, Colo.: Libraries Unlimited, 1986.
    Included in this book is a section on La Llorona along with some variants.

Melrose, Frances. "Tales of the Ghostly La Llorona Pre-date Cortez." *Rocky Mountain News* (Denver, Colorado). Sunday, January 21, 1990, 22-M.
    Melrose gives some background on the La Llorona story.

Storm, Hyemeyohsts. *Seven Arrows*. New York: Ballantine, 1972.
    This includes the story of Jumping Mouse, untitled, found on pages 68-85.

Notes

1. Bruno Bettelheim, *The Uses of Enchantment: The Meaning and Importance of Fairy Tales* (New York: Knopf, 1976), 23.
2. Ibid., 309.
3. Hyemeyohsts Storm, *Seven Arrows* (New York: Ballantine Books, 1972), 68-85.
4. Norma J. Livo and Sandra A. Rietz, *Storytelling: Process and Practice* (Littleton, Colo.: Libraries Unlimited, 1986), 240.
5. Ibid., 238-41.
6. Norma J. Livo, "Bogeyman (or Woman) Stories," *Yarnspinner* 17 (August 1993): 5-7.
7. Vi Hilbert, ed. and trans., *Haboo* (Seattle: University of Washington Press, 1985), 19-22, 42-44, 108-10, 150-51.

Helping Children Cope with Their Fears

The King's Son Who Feared Nothing
(collected by Jacob Grimm and Wilhelm Grimm)

Once there was a king's son who was no longer content to stay at home in his father's house. Since he had no fear of anything, he thought: I will go forth into the wide world. There the time will not seem long to me, and I shall see wonders enough. So he took leave of his parents and went forth—on and on from morning till night. Whichever way his path led it was the same to him.

It came to pass that he got to the house of a giant, and as he was so tired he sat down by the door and rested. And as he let his eyes roam here and there, he saw the giant's playthings lying in the yard. These were a couple of enormous balls and ninepins as tall as a man. After a while he fancied to set the ninepins up and then rolled the balls at them. He screamed and cried out when the ninepins fell and had a merry time of it.

The giant heard the noise, stretched his head out of the window, and saw a man who was not taller than other men and yet played with his ninepins. "Little worm!" cried he. "Why art thou playing with my ninepins? Who gave thee strength to do it?" The king's son looked up, saw the giant, and said: "Oh, thou blockhead, thou thinkest indeed that thou only hast strong arms. I can do everything I want to do."

The giant came down and watched the bowling with great admiration and said, "Child of man, if thou art one of that kind, go and bring me an apple of the tree of life."

"What dost thou want with it?" asked the king's son.

1

"I do not want the apple for myself," answered the giant, "but I have a betrothed bride who wishes for it. I have traveled far about the world and cannot find the tree."

"I will soon find it," said the king's son, "and I do not know what is to prevent me from getting the apple down."

The giant said: "Thou really believest it to be so easy! The garden in which the tree stands is surrounded by an iron railing, and in front of the railing lie wild beasts, each close to the other, and they keep watch and let no man go in."

"They will be sure to let me in," said the king's son.

"Yes, but even if thou dost get into the garden, and seest the apple hanging to the tree," said the giant, "it is still not thine. A ring hangs in front of it, through which any one who wants to reach the apple and break it off must put his hand. No one has yet had the luck to do it."

"That luck will be mine," said the king's son.

Then he took leave of the giant and went forth over mountain and valley and through plains and forests, until at length he came to the wondrous garden.

The beasts lay round about it, but they had put their heads down and were asleep. Moreover, they did not awaken when he went up to them, so he stepped over them, climbed the fence, and got safely into the garden. There, in the very middle of it, stood the tree of life, and the red apples were shining upon the branches. He climbed up the trunk to the top, and as he was about to reach out for an apple, he saw a ring hanging before it. He thrust his hand through the ring without any difficulty and gathered the apple. The ring closed tightly on his arm, and all at once he felt a prodigious strength flowing through his veins.

When he came down again from the tree with the apple, he did not climb over the fence but grasped the great gate and had no need to shake it more than once before it sprang open with a loud crash. Then he went out, and the lion, which had been lying down before, was awake and sprang after him, not in range and fierceness but following him humbly as if the king's son was his master.

The king's son took the giant the apple he had promised him and said, "Seest thou, I have brought it without difficulty." The giant, glad that his desire had been so soon satisfied, hastened to his bride, and gave her the apple for which she had wished. She was a beautiful and wise maiden, and as she did not see the ring on his arm, she said, "I shall never believe that thou hast brought the apple until I see the ring on thine arm."

The giant said, "I have nothing to do but go home and fetch it." He thought it would be easy to take away by force from the weak man what he would not give of his own free will. He therefore demanded the ring from him, but the king's son refused to give it to him. "Where the apple is, the ring must be also," said the giant. "If thou wilt not give it of thine own accord, thou must fight with me for it."

They wrestled with each other for a long time, but the giant could not get the better of the king's son, who was strengthened by the magical power of the ring. Then the giant thought of a stratagem, and said, "I have got warm fighting, and so hast thou. We will bathe in the river and cool ourselves before we begin again."

The king's son, who knew nothing of falsehood, went with him to the water and with his clothes along pulled off the ring from his arm and sprang into the river. The giant instantly snatched the ring and ran away with it, but the lion, which had observed the theft, pursued the giant, tore the ring out of his hand, and took it back to its master. Then the giant placed himself behind an oak tree, and while the king's son was busy putting on his clothes again the giant surprised him and put both his eyes out.

The unhappy king's son stood there and was blind and knew not how to help himself. Then the giant came back to him, took him by the hand as if he were someone who wanted to guide him, and led him to the top of a high rock. There he left him standing, and the giant thought, Just two steps more and he will fall down and kill himself, and I can take the ring from him. But the faithful lion had not deserted its master. It held him fast by his clothes and drew him gradually back to safety again.

When the giant returned to rob the man whom he felt sure would be dead, he saw that his cunning had been in vain. Is there no way, then, of destroying a weak child of man like that? he said angrily to himself, and he seized the king's son and led him back again to the precipice by another way. But the lion, who saw his evil design, helped its master out of danger there also. When they got close to the edge, the giant let the blind man's hand drop and was going to leave him behind alone, but the lion pushed the giant so that he fell and was dashed to pieces on the ground.

The faithful animal again drew its master back from the precipice and guided him to a tree by which flowed a clear brook. The king's son sat down there, but the lion lay down and sprinkled the water in his face with its paws. Scarcely had a couple of drops wet the sockets of his eyes before he was once more able to see something and remarked a little bird flying quite close by, which wounded itself against the trunk of the tree. It went down to the water and bathed itself therein, and then it soared upward and swept between the trees without touching them as if it had recovered its sight. Then the king's son recognized a sign from God and stooped down to the water and washed and bathed his face in it. And when he arose, he had his eyes once more—brighter and clearer than they had ever been.

The king's son thanked God for his great mercy and traveled with his lion onward through the world. And it came to pass that he arrived before a castle that was enchanted. In the gateway stood a maiden of beautiful form and fine face, but she was quite black. She spoke to him and said, "Ah, if thou couldst but deliver me from the evil spell that is thrown over me."

"What shall I do?" asked the king's son.

The maiden answered: "Thou must pass three nights in the great hall of this enchanted castle, but thou must let no fear enter thy heart. When they are doing their worst to torment thee, thou must bearest it without letting a sound escape thee, and I shall be free. Thy life they dare not take."

Then said the king's son, "I have no fear; with God's help I will try it."

So he went gaily into the castle, and when it grew dark, he seated himself in the large hall and waited. Everything was quiet, however, until midnight, when all at once a great tumult began, and out of every hole and corner came little devils. They behaved as if they did not see him, seated themselves in the middle of the room, lit a fire, and began to gamble. When one of them lost, he said: "It is not right. Someone is here who does not belong to us. It is his fault that I am losing."

"Wait, you fellow behind the stove, I am coming," said another.

The screaming became still louder. No one could have heard it without terror. The king's son stayed sitting quite quietly and was not afraid, but at last the devils jumped up from the ground and fell on him, and there were so many of them that he could not defend himself. They dragged him about on the floor, pinched him, pricked him, beat him, and tormented him, but no sound escaped from him.

Toward morning they disappeared, and he was so exhausted that he could scarcely move his limbs, but when day dawned the black maiden came to him. She bore in her hand a little bottle wherein was the water of life with which she washed him, and he at once felt all pain depart and new strength flow through his veins. She said, "Thou hast held out successfully for one night, but two more lie before thee." Then she went away again, and as she was going he observed that her feet had become white.

The next night the devils came and began their gambling anew. They fell on the king's son and beat him much more severely than the night before until his body was covered with wounds. But as he bore all quietly, they were forced to leave him, and when dawn appeared, the maiden came and healed him with the water of life. And when she went away, he saw with joy that she had already become white to the tips of her fingers.

Now he had only one night more to go through, but it was the worst. The hobgoblins came again. "Art thou there still?" cried they. "Thou shalt be tormented till thy breath stops." They pricked him and beat him and threw him here and there and pulled him by the arms and legs as if they wanted to tear him to pieces, but he bore everything and never uttered a cry. At last the devils vanished, but he lay fainting there and did not stir nor could he raise his eyes to look at the maiden who came in and sprinkled and bathed him with the water of life. But suddenly he was freed from all pain and felt fresh and healthy as if he had awakened from sleep. When he opened his eyes, he saw the maiden standing by him—snow-white and fair as day. "Rise," said she, "and swing thy sword three times over the stairs, and then all will be delivered."

And when he had done that, the whole castle was released from enchantment, and the maiden was revealed to be a rich king's daughter. The servants came up and said that the table was already set in the great hall, and dinner served up. Then they sat down and ate and drank together, and in the evening the wedding was solemnized with great rejoicings.

The Terrible Head

(collected by Jacob Grimm and Wilhelm Grimm)

Once upon a time there was a king whose only child was a girl. Now the king had been very anxious to have a son, or at least a grandson, to come after him, but he was told by a prophet whom he consulted that his own daughter's son should kill him. This news terrified him so much that he determined never to let his daughter be married, for he thought it was better to have no grandson at all than to be killed by his grandson. He therefore called his workmen together and bade them dig a deep round hole in the earth, and then he had a prison of brass built in the hole, and then, when it was finished, he locked up his daughter. No man ever saw her, and she never saw even the fields and the sea, but only the sky and the sun, for there was a wide-open window in the roof of the house of brass. So the princess would sit looking up at the sky and watching the clouds float across and would wonder whether she should ever get out of her prison. Now one day it seemed to her that the sky opened above her, and a great shower of shining gold fell through the window in the roof and lay glittering in her room. Not very long after, the princess had a baby—a little boy—but when her father the king heard of it, he was very angry and afraid, for now the child was born that should be his death. Yet, cowardly as he was, he had not quite the heart to kill the princess and her baby outright, but he had them put in a huge brass-bound chest and thrust out to sea so that they might either be drowned or starved or perhaps go to a country where they would be out of his way.

So the princess and the baby floated and drifted in the chest on the sea all day and all night, but the baby was not afraid of the waves nor of the wind, for he did not know that they could hurt him, and he slept quite soundly. And the princess sang a song over him, and this was her song:

Child, my child, how sound you sleep!
Though your mother's care is deep,
You can lie with heart at rest
In the narrow brass-bound chest;
In the starless night and drear
You can sleep, and never hear
Billows breaking, and the cry
Of the night-wind wandering by;
In soft purple mantle sleeping
  With your little face on mine,
Hearing not your mother weeping
  And the breaking of the brine.

Well, the daylight came at last, and the great chest was driven by the waves against the shore of an island. There the brass-bound chest lay, with the princess and her baby in it, till a man of that country came past and saw it and dragged it onto the beach, and when he had broken it open—behold!—there was a beautiful lady and a little boy. So he took them home and was very kind to them and brought up the boy till he was a young man. Now when the boy had come to his full strength, the king of that country fell in love with his mother and wanted to marry her, but he knew that she would never part from her boy. So he thought of a plan to get rid of the boy, and this was his plan. A great queen of a country not far off was going to be married, and this king said that all his subjects must bring him wedding presents to give her. And he made a feast to which he invited them all, and they all brought their presents. Some brought gold cups, and some brought necklaces of gold and amber, and some brought beautiful horses. But the boy had nothing, though he was the son of a princess, for his mother had nothing to give him. Then the rest of the company began to laugh at him, and the king said, "If you have nothing else to give, at least you might go and fetch the Terrible Head."

The boy was proud, and spoke without thinking: "Then I swear that I *will* bring the Terrible Head, if it may be brought by a living man. But of what head you speak I know not."

Then they told him that somewhere, a long way off, there dwelt three dreadful sisters—monstrous ogreish women—with golden wings and claws of brass and with serpents growing on their heads instead of hair. Now these women were so awful to look on that whoever saw them was turned at once into stone. And two of them could not be put to death, but the youngest, whose face was very beautiful, could be killed, and it was *her* head that the boy had promised to bring. You may imagine it was no easy adventure.

When he heard all this, he was perhaps sorry that he had sworn to bring the Terrible Head, but he was determined to keep his oath. So he went out from the feast, where they all sat drinking and making merry, and he walked alone beside the sea in the dusk of the evening at the place where the great chest, with himself and his mother in it, had been cast ashore.

There he went and sat down on a rock, looking toward the sea and wondering how he should begin to fulfill his vow. Then he felt someone touch him on the shoulder, and he turned and saw a young man like a king's son, having with him a tall and beautiful lady, whose blue eyes shone like stars. They were taller than mortal men, and the young man had a staff in his hand with golden wings on it and two golden serpents twisted round it, and he had wings on his cap and on his shoes. He spoke to the boy and asked him why he was so unhappy. The boy told him how he had sworn to take back the Terrible Head, and knew not how to begin to set about the adventure.

Then the beautiful lady also spoke and said that "it was a foolish oath and a hasty one, but it might be kept if a brave man had sworn it." Then the boy answered that he was not afraid if only he knew the way.

Then the lady said that to kill the dreadful woman with the golden wings and the brass claws, and to cut off her head, he needed three things: first, a Cap of Darkness, which would make him invisible when he wore it; next, a Sword of Sharpness, which would cleave iron at one blow; and last, the Shoes of Swiftness, with which he might fly in the air.

The boy answered that he knew not where such things were to be procured, and that, wanting them, he could only try and fail. Then the young man, taking off his own shoes, said: "First, you shall use these shoes till you have taken the Terrible Head, and then you must give them back to me. And with these shoes you will fly as fleet as a bird, or a thought, over the land or over the waves of the sea, wherever the shoes know the way. But there are ways that they do not know, roads beyond the borders of the world. And these roads have you to travel. Now first you must go to the Three Grey Sisters, who live far off in the north and are so very old that they have only one eye and one tooth among the three. You must creep up close to them, and as one of them passes the eye to the other you must seize it and refuse to give it up till they have told you the way to the Three Fairies of the Garden, and *they* will give you the Cap of Darkness and the Sword of Sharpness and show you how to wing beyond this world to the land of the Terrible Head."

Then the beautiful lady said: "Go forth at once, and do not return to say good-bye to your mother, for these things must be done quickly, and the Shoes of Swiftness themselves will carry you to the land of the Three Grey Sisters—for they know the measure of that way."

So the boy thanked her, and he fastened on the Shoes of Swiftness and turned to say good-bye to the young man and the lady. But—behold!—they had vanished. He knew not how or where! Then he leapt in the air to try the Shoes of Swiftness, and they carried him more swiftly than the wind, over the warm blue sea, over the happy lands of the south, over the northern peoples who drank mare's milk and lived in great wagons as they wandered after their flocks. Across the wide rivers, where the wild fowl rose and fled before him, and over the plains and the cold North Sea he went, over the fields of snow and the hills of ice, to a place where the world ends and all water is frozen, and there are no men nor beasts nor any green grass. There in a blue cave of the ice he found the Three Grey Sisters, the oldest of living things. Their hair was as white as the snow and their flesh an icy blue. And they mumbled and nodded in a kind of dream, and their frozen breath hung round them like a cloud. Now the opening of the cave in the ice was narrow, and it was not easy to pass in without touching one of the Grey Sisters. But, floating on the Shoes of Swiftness, the boy just managed to steal in, and waited till one of the sisters said to another, who had their one eye: "Sister, what do you see? Do you see old times coming back?"

"No, sister."

"Then give *me* the eye, for perhaps I can see farther than you."

Then the first sister passed the eye to the second, but as the second groped for it the boy caught it cleverly out of her hand.

"Where is the eye, sister?" asked the second grey woman.

"You have taken it yourself, sister," said the first grey woman.

"Have you lost the eye, sister? Have you lost the eye?" asked the third grey woman. "Shall we *never* find it again and see old times coming back?"

Then the boy slipped from behind them out of the cold cave into the air, and he laughed aloud.

When the grey women heard that laugh, they began to weep, for now they knew that a stranger had robbed them and that they could not help themselves, and their tears froze as they fell from the hollows where no eyes were and rattled on the icy ground of the cave. Then they began to implore the boy to give them their eye back again, and he could not help being sorry for them. They were so pitiful. But he said he would never give them the eye till they told him the way to the Three Fairies of the Garden.

Then they wrung their hands miserably, for they guessed why he had come and how he was going to try to win the Terrible Head. Now the Dreadful Women were akin to the Three Grey Sisters, and it was hard for them to tell the boy the way. But at last they told him to keep always south—with the land on his left and the sea on his right—till he reached the Island of the Three Fairies of the Garden. Then he gave them back the eye, and they began to look out once more for the old times coming back again. But the boy flew south between sea and land, keeping the land always on his left hand, till he saw a beautiful island crowned with flowering trees. There he alighted, and there he found the Three Fairies of the Garden. They were like three very beautiful young women, dressed one in green, one in white, and one in red, and they were dancing and singing round an apple tree with apples of gold, and this was their song:

The Song of the Western Fairies

Round and round the apples of gold,
  Round and round dance we;
Thus do we dance from the days of old
  About the enchanted tree;
Round, and round, and round we go,
While the spring is green, or the stream shall flow,
  Or the wind shall stir the sea!

There is none may taste of the golden fruit
  Till the golden new times come;
Many a tree shall spring from shoot,
Many a blossom be withered at root,
  Many a song be dumb;
Broken and still shall be many a lute
  Or ever the new times come!

Round and round the tree of gold,
  Round and round dance we,
So doth the great world spin from of old,
Summer and winter, and fire and cold,
Song that is sung, and tale that is told,
Even as we dance, that fold and unfold
  Round the stem of the fairy tree!

These grave dancing fairies were very unlike the Grey Sisters, and they were glad to see the boy and treated him kindly. Then they asked him why he had come, and he told them how he was sent to find the Sword of Sharpness and the Cap of Darkness. And the fairies gave him these and a wallet and a shield, and they belted the sword, which had a diamond blade, round his waist, and the cap they set on his head and told him that now even they could not see him though they were fairies. Then he took it off, and they each kissed him and wished him good fortune, and then they began again their eternal dance round the golden tree, for it is their business to guard it till the new times come or till the world's ending. So the boy put the cap on his head and hung the wallet round his waist and the shining shield on his shoulders and flew beyond the great river that lies coiled like a serpent round the whole world. And by the banks of that river he found the three Terrible Women all asleep beneath a poplar tree, and the dead poplar leaves lay all about them. Their golden wings were folded, and their brass claws were crossed. Two of them slept with their hideous heads beneath their wings like birds, and the serpents in their hair writhed out from under the feathers of gold. But the youngest slept between her two sisters, and she lay on her back, with her beautiful sad face turned to the sky, and though she slept her eyes were wide open. If the boy had seen her, he would have been changed into stone by the terror and the pity of it—she was so awful. But he had thought of a plan for killing her without looking on her face. As soon as he caught sight of the three from far off he took his shining shield from his shoulders and held it up like a mirror so that he saw the Dreadful Women reflected in it but did not see the Terrible Head itself. Then he came nearer and nearer, till he reckoned that he was within a sword's stroke of the youngest, and he guessed where he should strike a back blow behind him. Then he drew the Sword of Sharpness and struck once, and the Terrible Head was cut from the shoulders of the creature, and the blood leapt out and struck him like a blow. But he thrust the Terrible Head into his wallet, and flew away without looking behind. Then the two Dreadful Sisters who were left awakened and rose in the air like great birds. Though they could not see him because of his Cap of Darkness, they flew after him up the wind, following by the scent through the clouds like hounds hunting in a wood. They came so close that he could hear the clatter of their golden wings and their shrieks to each other as they chased him: "Here, here." "No there. This way he went." But the Shoes of Swiftness flew too fast for them, and at last their cries and the rattle of their wings died away as he crossed the great river that runs round the world.

Now when the horrible creatures were far in the distance and the boy found himself on the right side of the river, he flew straight eastward, trying to seek his own country. But as he looked down from the air he saw a very strange sight—a beautiful girl chained to a stake at the high-water mark of the sea. The girl was so frightened or so tired that she was only prevented from falling by the iron chain about her waist, and there she hung, as if she were dead. The boy was very sorry for her and flew down and stood beside her. When he spoke, she raised her head and looked round, but his voice only seemed to frighten her. Then he remembered that he was wearing the Cap of Darkness, and that she could only hear him, not see him. So he took it off, and there he stood before her, the handsomest young man she had ever seen in all her life, with short curly yellow hair and blue eyes and a laughing face. And he thought her the most beautiful girl in the world. So first with one blow of the Sword of Sharpness he cut the iron chain that bound her, and then he asked her what she did here and why men treated her so cruelly. And she told him that she was the daughter of the king of that country and that she was tied there to be eaten by a monstrous beast out of the sea; for the beast came and devoured a girl every day. Now the lot had fallen on her; and as she was just saying this a long fierce head of a cruel sea creature rose out of the waves and snapped at the girl. But the beast had been too greedy and too hurried, so he missed his aim the first time. Before he could rise and bite again, the boy whipped the Terrible Head out of his wallet and held it up. And when the sea beast leapt out once more, its eyes fell on the head, and instantly it was turned into a stone. And the stone beast is there on the seacoast to this day.

Then the boy and the girl went to the palace of the king, her father, where everyone was weeping for her death, and they could hardly believe their eyes when they saw her come back well. And the king and queen made much of the boy and could not contain themselves for delight when they found he wanted to marry their daughter. So the two were married with the most splendid rejoicings, and when they had passed some time at court, they went home in a ship to the boy's own country. For he could not carry his bride through the air, so he took the Shoes of Swiftness and the Cap of Darkness and the Sword of

Sharpness up to a lonely place in the hills. There he left them, and there they were found by the man and woman who had met him at home beside the sea, and who had helped him to start on his journey.

When this had been done, the boy and his bride set forth for home and landed at the harbor of his native land. But whom should he meet in the very street of the town but his own mother, flying for her life from the wicked king, who now wished to kill her because he found that she would never marry him! For if she had liked the king ill before, she liked him far worse now that he had caused her son to disappear so suddenly. She did not know, of course, where the boy had gone, but thought the king had slain him secretly. So now she was running for her very life, and the wicked king was following her with a sword in his hand. Then—behold!—she ran into her son's very arms, but he had only time to kiss her and step in front of her when the king struck at him with his sword. The boy caught the blow on his shield, and cried to the king, "I swore to bring you the Terrible Head, and see how I keep my oath!"

Then he drew forth the head from his wallet, and when the king's eyes fell on it, instantly he was turned into stone, just as he stood there with his sword lifted!

Now all the people rejoiced, because the wicked king should rule them no longer. And they asked the boy to be their king, but he said no, he must take his mother home to her father's house. So the people chose for king the man who had been kind to his mother when first she was cast on the island in the great chest.

Presently the boy and his mother and his wife set sail for his mother's own country, from which she had been driven so unkindly. But on the way they stayed at the court of a king, and it happened that he was holding games and giving prizes to the best runners, boxers, and quoit throwers. Then the boy would try his strength with the rest, but he threw the quoit so far that it went beyond what had been thrown before and fell in the crowd, striking a man so that he died. Now this man was no other than the father of the boy's mother, who had fled away from his own kingdom for fear his grandson should find him and kill him after all. Thus he was destroyed by his own cowardice and by chance, and thus the prophecy was fulfilled. But the boy and his wife and his mother went back to the kingdom that was theirs and lived long and happily after all their troubles.

(Reprinted by permission of the publisher.)

Discussion

The king's son and the boy were not like the rest of us. They knew no or little fear and therefore everything was possible. Many adults take the fears of children lightly and even treat them jokingly. One afternoon I had my four-year-old grandson in the school playground. There was a geodesic jungle gym there, and I could see that he dearly wanted to try it. However, he hesitated and asked me, "Grandmother, will I be afraid?" I answered, "Well, Todd, try it and then tell me if you were." He tentatively started climbing and swinging and enjoyed himself. As we were leaving I asked him, "Were you afraid?" His answer was, "Of what?" He had already forgotten that that new experience might have been fearful. He had mastered the equipment and with that any idea of fear.

We all remember fears of our childhood. One family member raised in a log house in northern Canada remembered the noises the stairs made on cold nights. It sounded like someone was sneaking down from upstairs. When he heard the sounds, he hid deeper in his sheepskin cover. I remember three huge buckeye trees outside my bedroom window. In the winter when their leaves were gone, the stark branches scraped against the house and windows, making weird sounds and looking spooky in the moonlight. Then there were the times a particular uncle came to visit who snored—not just little snores but snores that rattled the walls. His snores became part of my nightmares, which involved attacking bears. I never told my parents about the sleep I lost when Uncle Rube visited. I guess I thought they already knew.

Adults might be surprised to learn what children actually say they fear. One study, "Voices in Unison: Stressful Events in the Lives of Children in Six Countries," conducted by Kaoru Yamamoto, Abdalla Soliman, James Parsons, and O. L. Davies, Jr., found that adults and children appear to know amazingly little about one another.

The researchers tried to find out how the world appears to the youngsters of six countries. The children studied were third- through ninth-graders from Egypt, Canada, Australia, Japan, Philippines, and the United States. Each child was given a list of 20 stressful events and asked to rate how unpleasant the event would be on a scale of one (the least upsetting) to seven (the most upsetting). The 20 events, ranked in order, that the children found stressful and fear the most are:

- losing a parent
- going blind
- being retained academically
- urinating in class
- fighting by parents
- being caught in theft
- being suspected of lying
- having a poor report card
- being sent to principal
- having an operation
- getting lost
- being ridiculed in class
- moving to a new school
- having a scary dream
- not making 100 on a test
- being picked last on team
- losing in a game
- going to the dentist
- giving a class report
- having a new baby sibling

In earlier studies, child experts, teachers, and college students were asked to rate the same 20 stressful events according to how stressful they believed each would be for a child. The adults rated "having a new brother or sister" as the most stressful event for children, while the children themselves rated it as least stressful. In fact, adults rated stressful events differently from the children in 16 of the 20 categories. Yamamoto said, "For two people who have lived side by side for such a long time, the adult and the child appear to know amazingly little about each other." The researchers found that boys and girls have the same fears and that variations among grades were essentially nonexistent. They were amazed to observe the close parallels among the children's assessments of life events across different cultures. Yamamoto concluded, "If this culture of the young overlaps relatively little with that of the grown-ups, it behooves us to pay closer attention to the structure and function of the childhood, as seen from the inside."

It would seem from the children's list of stressful events, that school life is a trying thing for them. The researchers discovered a reported prevalence of belittling practices by adults toward children. This underscores that embarrassment or humiliation is an especially stinging blow to a child's emerging sense of worth. Children should be treated with respect as well as afforded experiences and situations that contribute to positive self-esteem.

Psychologists and educators have suggested several approaches to help children overcome and cope with the normal fears of childhood. Generally it is recommended that adults 1) reassure the child, 2) discuss fears with the child to reduce the child's feelings of isolation, 3) give the child accurate information about his or her fears, which are often irrational and based on misinformation or misinterpretation, 4) reinforce the child's efforts to manage his or her own fears, and 5) give bounteous praise to reward the smallest evidence of courage in children of any age. (When children take the step to overcome the thumping of their hearts and their uncertainty—whether successful or not—they deserve praise for that attempt.)

Jack Zipes in *The Trials and Tribulations of Little Red Riding Hood* argues that the essence of our lives has been prescribed and circumscribed by fairy tales. He explores in depth the uses of Little Red Riding Hood. Clarissa Pinkola Estes in *Women Who Run with the Wolves* establishes that women need to reconnect with the healthy, instinctual attributes to be found in the archetype of the wild woman. She feels that without the wild woman, women become overdomesticated, fearful, uncreative, and trapped. She uses myths and stories along with discussion to point out the needs of women.

Stories can be effective in helping to diminish children's fears. Bruno Bettelheim, the child psychiatrist, considered this whole area in his benchmark book *The Uses of Enchantment: Meaning and Importance of Fairy Tales.* In this book, he develops the need for children to develop inner resources in order to cope with difficult problems. He states that "nothing in the entire range of children's literature can be as enriching and satisfying to child and adult alike as the folk fairy tale."[1] He felt that children were able to face frightening life experiences after they had safely seen story characters handle danger.

That is precisely what this book hopes to address. What books and stories and activities are useful to help children master their fears? I will address each of the children's listed fears and provide resources for guidance. We must also recognize that stories cannot be applied like a bandage: There must be respectful and caring concern for the child. Fears can be reduced, and that will produce emotional healing as well as possibly provide some preventative interventions.

Activities

- After reading or telling the story of "The King's Son Who Feared Nothing" or "The Terrible Head" discuss with the children whether having no fear can be dangerous. If so, when and why could it be dangerous?

- Have the children speculate as to how the king's son and the boy coped with the ill treatment. This could be helpful because there are children who must deal with this kind of behavior from parents, siblings, and peers.

- Ask youngsters to share what they are afraid of. What do they remember made them afraid? Did they get over some of their fears? If so, how did they do that?

- Ask the children whether talking about what they fear helps them in their worries about their fears or does it make things worse? Sometimes finding out that others have had fears about the same things can help take away some of the intensity. It is when people think they are alone in something that it has more power over them.

- Have the children sift through some folk stories and analyze what fears the story characters cope with.

The following is a listing of children's fears in alphabetical order. Copy this list for a parent or teacher workshop, and give it to the participants. Ask them to read the items according to what they think children fear the most. Then compare their predictions with the actual order as given by children. Which fears differed? What are the implications of these differences?

- being blind
- being kept back a grade
- caught in theft
- getting lost
- giving a class report

- going to a dentist
- having an operation
- losing a parent (to death or divorce)
- losing in a game
- moving to a new school
- new baby sibling
- not making 100 on a test
- parental fights
- picked last on the team
- poor report card
- ridiculed in class
- scary dream
- sent to the principal
- suspected of lying
- wetting in class

Bibliography

Grimm, Jacob, and Wilhelm Grimm. "The Youth Who Could Not Shiver and Shake." In *Grimm's Complete Fairy Tales.* Garden City, N.Y.: Doubleday, n.d.

A father has two sons. The oldest son, Jack, is smart and can do anything. However, he is a terrible coward. His younger brother is considered stupid and has no fears. The younger brother sets out from his home to learn how to shiver and shake. He learns about that but not about fear.

Ingpen, Robert. *The Age of Acorns.* New York: Peter Bedrick, 1990.

A toy bear is left outside in the garden and eventually retrieved after dark. Bear sees terrifying visions from his lookout position in the old oak tree. Even though Bear is retrieved and the gruesome entourage disappears, Bear cannot help thinking about what happened and what might have happened. There is the familiar pattern of abandonment, recovery, and consolation, with the added suggestion that fears do not just go away. Even if we are safe from harm, we still shiver when we think of them.

Sendak, Maurice. *Pierre, a Cautionary Tale in Five Chapters and a Prologue.*
   New York: Harper & Row, 1962.
   In this delightful book Pierre refuses to cooperate with his parents and answers everything with "I don't care." When a lion comes Pierre answers his questions with "I don't care," but the lion teaches him that maybe he does care after all.

Zipes, Jack. *Spells of Enchantment.* New York: Viking, 1991.
   A comprehensive collection of fairy tales of western culture.

References

Bettelheim, Bruno. *The Uses of Enchantment: Meaning and Importance of Fairy Tales.* New York: Knopf, 1976.
   Bettelheim discusses how fairy tales help children to make orderly their tumultuous feelings. He also feels that children abstract ethical concepts and meanings as they listen to these stories.

Estes, Clarissa Pinkola. *Women Who Run with the Wolves.* New York: Ballantine, 1992.
   In her best-selling book, Estes presents myths and stories along with psychological discussion of the wild-woman archetype.

Yamamoto, Kaoru, Abdalla Soliman, James Parsons, and O. L. Davies, Jr. "Voices in Unison: Stressful Events in the Lives of Children in Six Countries." *Journal of Child Psychology and Psychiatry* 28, no. 6 (1987): 855-64.

Zipes, Jack. *The Trials and Tribulations of Little Red Riding Hood.* South Hadley, Mass.: Bergin and Garvey, 1983.
   Zipes discusses manners and norms and explores the use of Little Red Riding Hood during the seventeenth century to reinforce the civilizing process.

Note

1. Bruno Bettelheim, *The Uses of Enchantment: The Meaning and Importance of Fairy Tales* (New York: Knopf, 1976), 309.

Truth

(traditional story from the Far East)

One day the gods decided to create the universe. They created stars, the sun, and the moon. They created the seas, mountains, flowers, trees, and clouds. They created human beings. After everything in the universe had been created, they created Truth. They weren't sure where they should place Truth. They wanted it to be somewhere where people would not find it right away. They wanted to make sure people had to search for Truth. And so they considered putting it on the highest mountain, the farthest star, the deepest and darkest abyss or concealing it on the secret side of the moon. Finally the gods decided to put Truth inside the human heart so that people would search throughout the universe for it and only find it when they looked within.

The Mouse and the Lion

(a retelling of an Aesop fable)

By Sharon Creeden

There once was a mouse—a small mouse—quick and quiet and gray. He lived in a jungle—a huge, wild jungle where all the animals were fierce. So he tried to stay out of everyone's way.

One day the mouse was scurrying across the floor of the jungle and ran into a paw. It was a huge, furry yellow paw. And suddenly the paw picked up the mouse by his tail and held him high in the air. The paw belonged to a huge, furry yellow lion.

"Well, hello, Little Mouthful," said the lion. "You tickled my paw and woke me up. Too bad for you." The lion opened his mouth and lifted the mouse to drop him inside.

The lion's mouth looked as big as a cave. The teeth were long and sharp and white.

"Please," said the mouse, "do not eat me. I am sorry I woke you up."

"I don't mind waking up for something to eat," said the lion.

"You won't like me. I am very small and very bony," said the mouse.

"And I am not very hungry," said the lion. "I just had dinner. But you will make a munchy, crunchy after-naptime snack."

"Please," said the mouse. "If you don't eat me, I promise someday I will help you."

The lion smiled and then chuckled. "I am King Lion," he said. "What could you do for me?" He laughed and laughed to think that a small scared mouse could help him. "Oh, I love a good laugh," he said. "I don't think I'll eat you." He put the mouse on the ground and set him free. "Run fast, Little Mouthful," said the lion. And the mouse ran and ran.

Several weeks later, he heard the lion roaring in anger and fear.

He thought, King Lion is in trouble. I will keep my promise. He ran to help.

He saw the lion trapped by a hunter's net. The lion was rolling on the ground and ripping at the net with his claws. The mouse was afraid he would be crushed if he went near. When at last the lion lay weak and still, the mouse crept up to the lion's ear and said: "Remember me? You called me Little Mouthful, and you did not eat me. I will help you now."

The lion lay quiet. The mouse began to bite the net. His tiny sharp teeth were just right for chewing through ropes. He nibbled and nibbled until there was a hole in the net.

The lion crawled through the hole. He stood and stretched and gave a roar of freedom.

The mouse was frightened by the roar and ran into the jungle. King Lion called out: "Come back. I want to thank you."

The mouse came out of hiding and let King Lion pick him up.

King Lion said: "You are more than a snack. You are more than a wee bit of gray fur. You are a brave jungle animal. You are a friend. And you make me laugh." The lion laughed a tree-shaking laugh, and King Lion and Little Mouthful walked away together.

(Reprinted with permission of the author.)

Discussion

We talk about children's fears because we are concerned with their growing up, and stories are vital to this whole process of becoming whole human beings. Stories help shape our lives and society. We are all heroes of our own life stories and can identify with story characters who have made it through terrible difficulties to a successful ending. Seeing story characters with problems "make it" can help us believe that our problems are solvable.

Every culture and religion gives us stories to help us survive and flourish. They keep our human spirit renewed and full of courage. There is a predictable quality to stories that develops possibilities for us all. Children are no different. If children have learned the "grammar" of stories and are familiar with the structure of stories, they can build some courage and strength to help them face and conquer the ogres of our lives.

It is no coincidence that worldwide there are worldwide mythologies and folk stories that are filled with ogres and giants, because the world is an amazing place and trying to explain every natural happening in it is difficult. So we find giants everywhere wreaking havoc and magic and guides to help us survive. Ancient people, for example, explained thunder as the work of giants. There have also been people who have been larger than life, giantlike. Some were good giants, and others were not.

Children live in the world of giants. Have you ever been on an elevator with a small child and imagined the world from his or her point of view? It is filled with the legs, purses, and briefcases of giants with booming voices. Because children might develop a sense of helplessness and insecurity, they must be given the weapons to develop power and possibilities.

Those weapons come in stories. Stories help youngsters accept the thought that the weak and small can overcome. These stories should be influential so that they extend experiences through imagination. When successful, these stories become associated with energy and awareness and can call them back at will to deepen and control the memory. They arouse powerful feelings that can awaken insights deep within and give flashes of insight or intuition. They can help all of us grow and survive.

This front-page *Denver Post* newspaper story from Tuesday, January 31, 1978, proves the point about the power of stories. In Richfield, Minnesota, police said they were amazed at the courage and presence of mind of a tiny 11-year-old girl. The girl, an avid fan of Nancy Drew mysteries, was abducted, sexually molested in a garage, and put in the trunk of a 1970 Ford. Dressed in only a blouse and with a blanket wrapped around her, the 80-pound youngster spent more than 10 hours in the car. She unscrewed several bolts and escaped through a 12-x-6-inch taillight hole. She walked down the street, flagged down a car, and was taken to a police station. The police caught and charged a suspect by tracking down a car with the rear light missing. One of the officers said the girl's interest in mystery stories may have helped her believe she was capable of escaping. She had read as many as 45 Nancy Drew books and thought, What would Nancy Drew do? The officer continued, "It seems to have prepared her mind to deal with the situation and to escape."

What stories give us is truth, and that truth gives each person inspiration. It is that inspiration that helps us to cope.

Activities

- Have the children keep a file of stories that they find inspirational. Why do they have that quality for the children? What makes them inspirational?

- Identify story characters who are small and weak and helpless. Do they change in the course of the story? If so, how does the story show this change? For instance, the Br'er Rabbit stories revolve around the character of a (usually considered) small, weak rabbit who succeeds because of his cleverness, not his size or strength.

- Ask the children to tell or read one of the stories that they feel strongly about. What was there about this story that made it inspirational to them? Find out if others' reactions are the same or different.

- Encourage the children to write a story in which they are the hero. Past or current problems in their lives may serve as a basis. What journey can they take to try to solve these problems? How do the problems become resolved? (Remember most folk stories have a skeleton of story structure: A hero with a problem goes off to solve it. In stories of Western culture the hero usually has three tries to successfully and quickly resolve a problem. Sometimes there is a guide or helper.) The hero can reach the solution using trickery, wisdom, intelligence, kindness, or persistence.

- Visit a nursing home and collect stories that residents there find inspirational. What stories have helped them overcome difficulties? These stories could include fables, religious stories, folktales, or biographies. The collected stories could be sorted into categories and published. After publication, share the stories with the folks in the nursing home or place a copy in the school library.

- What pieces of music do the children find inspirational? Develop a chart of these musical selections and categorize them according to their attributes. Do some pieces fit under several categories?

Bibliography

Borden, Louise. *Albie the Lifeguard.* Illustrations by Elizabeth Sayles. New York: Scholastic, 1993.
This is the story of how one child conquers his fears through imagination.

Brown, Heywood. *The Fifty-First Dragon.* Illustrations by Ed Emberley. Englewood Cliffs, N.J.: Prentice Hall, 1968.
Gawaine le Coeur-Hardy is the least promising of all the pupils at the knight school. When assigned to slay dragons, Gawaine whimpers and begs for some magic to help him. His instructor gives him a magic word that will make dragons unable to harm him. Gawaine goes on to an illustrious career in dragon killing but grows sloppy in his work and one day forgets the magic word. He is confronted by a dragon and has no time to do anything except strike. When he asks his instructor how he managed the kill without the magic word, the instructor tells him that the word was not really magic. It only gave him confidence. With this truth, Gawaine loses his courage and is eaten by the 51st dragon.

Karl, Jean. *The Search for the Ten-Winged Dragon.* Illustrations by Steve Cieslawski. New York: Doubleday, 1990.
A young apprentice, Tobias, in the toy shop of A. Butterworth longs to make toys all by himself. The toy master contends that Tobias will not be ready for the task until he has learned the basic skills of the trade and seen a 10-winged dragon. Tobias's search for the fantastical creature leads him on a remarkable journey of adventure and self-discovery. Determination, courage, and imagination are special virtues in this story.

Kraus, Robert. *Leo the Late Bloomer*. Illustrations by Jose Aruego. New York: Dutton, 1971.

Leo the tiger is a late bloomer. His parents are concerned and seek help. They watch for signs of Leo changing and are surprised when one day he blooms just like he knew he would. Kraus, himself a late bloomer, wrote this for all the children and their parents to give them patience and hope.

Krauss, Ruth. *The Carrot Seed*. Illustrations by Crockett Johnson. New York: Harper & Row, 1945.

A little boy plants one carrot seed. Everyone in the family tells him it will not come up, but he continues to care for it. One day a carrot (giant size) comes up just as he knew it would.

Mathis, Sharon Bell. *The Hundred Penny Box*. Illustrations by Leo Dillon and Diane Dillon. New York: Viking, 1975.

Michael's love for his 100-year-old great-great-aunt Dew is very special. When they spend time together, Aunt Dew takes out her 100 penny box and tells him stories to go with the 100 pennies that represent the years in her life.

Piper, Watty. *The Little Engine That Could*. Illustrations by George Hauman and Doris Hauman. New York: Platt and Munk, 1954.

The classic story of the little engine that believed in itself and pulled the trainload of toys over the mountain.

"Real-Life Nancy Drew Flees Car Trunk." UPI. *Denver Post*. Tuesday, January 31, 1978 (vol. 86, no. 184), 1.

Shecter, Ben. *Conrad's Castle*. New York: Harper & Row, 1967.

Told with very few words, this book is the story of a youngster who loses confidence in something wonderful he is doing. It is a poignant tale and full of humor.

Steptoe, John. *The Story of Jumping Mouse*. New York: Lothrop, Lee & Shepard, 1984.

The smallest and humblest of creatures can dream of courage if faithful to himself and his dream. This story of the Plains Indians is told and illustrated with compassion and power.

Hansel and Gretel

(collected by Jacob Grimm and Wilhelm Grimm)

Near a great forest there lived a poor woodcutter and his wife and his two children by his dead first wife. The boy's name was Hansel and the girl's, Gretel. They had little to bite or to sup, and once, when there was a great dearth in the land, the man could not even gain the daily bread.

As he lay in bed one night thinking of this and turning and tossing, he sighed heavily and said to his wife: "What will become of us? We cannot even feed our children. There is nothing left for ourselves."

"I will tell you what, husband," answered the wife. "We will take the children early in the morning into the forest where it is thickest. We will make them a fire, and we will give each of them a piece of bread. Then we will go to our work and leave them alone. They will never find the way home again, and we shall be quit of them."

"No, wife," said the man. "I cannot do that. I cannot find it in my heart to take my children into the forest and leave them there alone. The wild animals would soon come and devour them."

"Oh, you fool," said she. "Then we will all four starve. You had better get the coffins ready." She left him no peace until he consented.

"But I really pity the poor children," said the man.

The two children had not been able to sleep for hunger and had heard what their stepmother had said to their father. Gretel wept bitterly and said to Hansel, "It is all over with us."

"Do be quiet, Gretel," said Hansel, "and do not fret. I will manage something."

When the parents had gone to sleep, he got up, put on his little coat, opened the back door, and slipped out. The moon was shining brightly, and the white flints that lay in front of the house glistened like pieces of silver. Hansel stooped and filled the little pockets of his coat as full as he could. Then he went back inside again and said to Gretel: "Be easy, dear little sister, and go to sleep quietly. God will not forsake us." And he laid himself down again in his bed.

When the day was breaking and before the sun had risen, the wife came and awakened the two children, saying: "Get up, you lazy bones. We are going into the forest to cut wood."

Then she gave each of them a piece of bread and said, "That is for dinner, and you must not eat it before then, for you will get no more."

Gretel carried the bread under her apron, for Hansel had his pockets full of the flints. Then they set off all together on their way to the forest. When they had gone a little way, Hansel stood still and looked back toward the house, and this he did again and again, till his father said to him: "Hansel, what are you looking at? Take care not to forget your legs."

"Oh, father," said Hansel, "I am looking at my little white kitten, who is sitting up on the roof to bid me good-bye."

"You young fool," said the woman. "That is not your kitten but the sunshine on the chimney pot."

Of course, Hansel had not been looking at his kitten but had been taking every now and then a flint, a hard dark stone, from his pocket and dropping it on the road.

When they reached the middle of the forest, the father told the children to collect wood to make a fire to keep them warm, and Hansel and Gretel gathered brushwood enough for a little mountain. They set it on fire, and when the flame was burning quite high the wife said: "Now lie down by the fire and rest yourselves, you children, and we will go and cut wood. When we are ready, we will come and fetch you."

So Hansel and Gretel sat by the fire, and at noon they each ate their pieces of bread. They thought their father was in the wood all the time, as they seemed to hear the strokes of the ax, but really it was only a dry branch hanging from a withered tree that the wind moved to and fro. So when they had stayed there a long time, their eyelids closed with weariness, and they fell fast asleep.

When at last they woke, it was night. Gretel began to cry, and she said, "How shall we ever get out of this wood?"

Hansel comforted her, saying, "Wait a little while longer, until the moon rises, and then we can easily find the way home."

And when the full moon got up, Hansel took his little sister by the hand and followed the way where the flint stones shone like silver and showed them the road. They walked on the whole night through, and at the break of day they came to their father's house. They knocked at the door, and when the wife opened it and saw it was Hansel and Gretel, she said: "You naughty children, why did you sleep so long in the wood? We thought you were never coming home again!" But the father was glad, for it had gone to his heart to leave them both in the woods alone.

Not very long after that there was again great scarcity in those parts, and the children heard their stepmother say at night in bed to their father: "Everything is finished up. We have only half a loaf, and after that the tale comes to an end. The children must be off. We will take them farther into the wood this time so that they shall not be able to find the way back again. There is no other way to manage."

The man felt sad at heart, and he thought, It would be better to share one's last morsel with one's children. But the wife would listen to nothing that he said. She scolded and reproached him. When a man has given in once, he has to do it a second time.

But the children were not asleep and had heard all the talk. So when the parents had gone to sleep, Hansel got up to go out and get some more flint stones as he had done before. But the wife had locked the door, and Hansel could not get out. He comforted his little sister and said: "Do not cry, Gretel. Go to sleep quietly, and God will help us."

Early the next morning the wife came and pulled the children out of bed. She gave them each a little piece of bread—less than before. On the way to the wood Hansel crumbled the bread in his pocket and often stopped to throw a crumb on the ground.

"Hansel, what are you stopping behind and staring for?" asked the father.

"I am looking at my little pigeon sitting on the roof and saying good-bye to me," answered Hansel.

"You fool," said the wife. "That is no pigeon but is the morning sun shining on the chimney pots."

Hansel went on as before and strewed bread crumbs all along the road.

The woman led the children far into the wood—farther than they had ever been before. And again they made a large fire, and the stepmother said: "Sit still there, you children. And when you are tired, you can go to sleep. We are going into the forest to cut wood, and in the evening when we are ready to go home, we will come and fetch you."

So when noon came, Gretel shared her bread with Hansel, who had strewed his along the road. Then they went to sleep, and the evening passed, and no one came for the poor children. When they awoke, it was dark night. Hansel comforted his little sister and said: "Wait a little, Gretel, until the moon gets up. Then we shall be able to see the way home by the crumbs of bread that I have scattered on the trail."

So when the moon rose, they got up, but they could find no crumbs of bread, for the birds of the woods and of the fields had come and picked them up. Hansel thought they might find the way all the same, but they could not. They went on all that night and the next day—from the morning until the evening—but they could not find the way out of the woods. They were very hungry, for they had nothing to eat but the few berries they could pick up. And when they were so tired that they could no longer drag themselves along, they lay down under a tree and fell asleep.

It was then the third morning since they had left their father's house. They tried to find their way back, but instead they only found themselves farther in the wood, and if help had not soon come, they would have starved. About noon they saw a pretty snow-white bird sitting on a bough and singing so sweetly that they stopped to listen. And when he had finished the bird spread his wings and flew before them, and they followed after him until they came to a little house. The bird perched on the roof, and when they came nearer, they saw that the house was built of bread and roofed with cakes. The window was of transparent sugar.

"We will have some of this," said Hansel, "and make a fine meal. I will eat a piece of the roof Gretel, and you can have some of the window—that will taste sweet."

So Hansel reached up and broke off a bit of the roof just to see how it tasted, and Gretel stood by the window and gnawed at it. Then they heard a thin voice call out from inside,

Nibble, nibble, like a mouse
Who is nibbling at my house?
And the children answered,
Never mind,
It is the wind.

And they went on eating, never disturbing themselves. Hansel, who found that the roof tasted very nice, took down a great piece of it, and Gretel pulled out a large, round windowpane. They sat themselves down and began to eat. Then the door opened and an aged woman came out, leaning on a crutch. Hansel and Gretel felt frightened and let fall what they had in their hands. The old woman, however, nodded her head and asked: "Ah, my dear children, how come you here? You must come indoors and stay with me. You will be no trouble."

So she took each by the hand and led them into her little house. There they found a good meal laid out of milk and pancakes with sugar, apples, and nuts. After they had eaten, the old woman showed them two little white beds, and Hansel and Gretel laid themselves down on them and thought they were in heaven.

The old woman, although her behavior was so kind, was a wicked witch, who lay in wait for children and had built the little house to entice them. When they were once inside, she used to kill them, cook them, and eat them, and then it was a feast day with her. The witch's eyes were red, and she could not see very far, but she had a keen scent, like the beasts, and knew very well when human creatures were near. When she had seen that Hansel and Gretel were coming, she had given a spiteful laugh and had said triumphantly, "I have them, and they shall not escape me!"

Early in the morning, before the children were awake, she got up to look at them. As they lay sleeping so peacefully with round rosy cheeks, she said to herself, What a fine feast I shall have!

Then she grasped Hansel with her withered hand and led him into a little stable and shut him up behind a grating. Call and scream as he might, it did no good. Then she went back to Gretel and shook her, crying, "Get up, lazy bones, fetch water and cook something nice for your brother. He is outside in the stable and must be fattened up. And when he is fat enough, I will eat him."

Gretel began to weep bitterly, but it was no use. She had to do what the wicked witch bade her.

And so the best kinds of victuals were cooked for poor Hansel, while Gretel got nothing but crab shells. Each morning the old woman visited the little stable and cried, "Hansel, stretch out your finger so that I may tell if you will soon be fat enough to eat."

Hansel, however, used to hold out a little bone, and the old woman, who had weak eyes, could not see what it was. Supposing it to be Hansel's finger, she wondered that it was not getting fatter. When four weeks had passed and Hansel seemed to remain so thin, she lost patience and could wait no longer.

"Now then, Gretel," cried she to the little girl. "Be quick and draw water. Be Hansel fat or be he lean, tomorrow I must kill and cook him."

Oh, what a grief for the poor little sister to have to fetch water, and how the tears flowed down over her cheeks! "Dear God, pray help us!" cried she. "If we had been devoured by wild beasts in the wood, at least we should have died together."

"Spare me your lamentations," said the old woman. "They are of no avail."

Early the next morning Gretel had to get up, make the fire, and fill the kettle. "First we will do the baking," said the old woman. "I have heated the oven already and kneaded the dough."

She pushed poor Gretel toward the oven, out of which the flames were already shining. "Creep in," said the witch, "and see if it is properly hot so that the bread may be baked."

With Gretel in the oven the witch meant to shut the door upon her and let her be baked, and then she would have eaten her. But Gretel perceived her intention and said: "I don't know how to do it. How shall I get in?"

"Stupid goose," said the old woman. "The opening is big enough, do you see? I could get in myself." And then she stooped down and put her head in the oven's mouth. Then Gretel gave her a push so that she went in farther, and she shut the iron door upon her and put up the bar. Oh, how frightfully the witch howled! But Gretel ran away and left the wicked witch to burn miserably. Gretel went straight to Hansel, opened the stable door, and cried: "Hansel, we are free! The old witch is dead!"

Then out flew Hansel like a bird from its cage as soon as the door was opened. How happy they both were! How they fell each on the other's neck and danced about and kissed each other! And as they had nothing more to fear, they went all over the old witch's house and found that in every corner there stood chests of pearls and precious stones.

"This is something better than flint stones," said Hansel as he filled his pockets. Gretel, thinking she also would like to carry something home with her, filled her apron full.

"Now, away we go," said Hansel. "If we only can get out of the witch's wood."

When they had journeyed a few hours, they came to a great piece of water. "We can never get across this," said Hansel. "I see no stepping-stones and no bridge."

"And there is no boat either," said Gretel. "But here comes a white duck. If I ask her, she will help us over." So Gretel cried,

Duck, duck, here we stand,
Hansel and Gretel, on the land,
Stepping-stones and bridge we lack,
Carry us over on your nice white back.

And the duck came accordingly, and Hansel got upon her and told his sister to come too. "No," answered Gretel, "that would be too hard upon the duck. We can go separately, one after the other."

And that was how it was managed, and after that they went on happily until they came to the wood. The way grew more and more familiar, till at last they saw in the distance their father's house. Then they ran till they came up to it, rushed in at the door, and fell on their father's neck. The man had not had a quiet hour since he had left his children in the wood. His wife was dead. When Gretel opened her apron, the pearls and precious stones were scattered all over the room, and Hansel took one handful after another out of his pocket. Then was all care at an end, and they lived in great joy together.

> *Sing every one*
> *My story is done,*
> *And look! round the house*
> *There runs a little mouse.*
> *He that can catch her before she scampers in*
> *May make himself a fur cap out of her skin.*

The Tale of the Oki Islands

(from Japan)

There once was a girl named Tokoyo who was dearly loved by her father, Oribe Shima. Oribe was a samurai, a soldier of great nobility. But he and his daughter had been separated when the emperor banished him after a misunderstanding. The emperor had suffered from ill health for many years and often acted in haste because of his discomfort. Oribe had been sent to the Oki Islands, a desolate set of islands off the coast of Japan. There Oribe passed lonely days, wondering what Tokoyo was doing and dreaming of his former life.

Tokoyo was an exceptionally brave girl. Her many years spent diving for oysters had made her strong and courageous. She decided she would no longer be separated from her father and sold nearly all her belongings so that she could go to him.

She arrived at the village of Akasaki and looked longingly across the sea to the distant islands where her father was exiled. She asked many fishermen to take her to the islands, but no one dared risk the anger of the emperor.

But Tokoyo would not be dissuaded. After buying a bit of food, she waited for nightfall. Then she stole down to the edge of the water and cut loose a small sailboat. All through the night and the next day she sailed across the sea until she arrived on the shore of one of the islands. Darkness was closing in, and she fell exhausted to the ground, where she slept through the night.

The next morning she started walking along the shore. She asked a fisherman about her father, and he cautioned her to never mention his name aloud or she would risk further retribution. Heeding his advice, she wandered from village to village, listening to the people's conversations, hoping to learn about her father. No one spoke of him.

After many days she came to a shrine high above the water where she prayed to Buddha for help. It was evening, and she dozed for some time, only to be awakened by the sound of a young girl's weeping. She looked around her and saw a priest praying over a lovely young girl who was dressed in a white robe. The priest led the sobbing girl to the high rocks and continued his prayers. Tokoyo crept up behind them, and just as the priest was about to push the girl over the rocks and into the sea below, Tokoyo grabbed her and pulled her back onto the rocks.

The priest was astounded at her actions and told her why he had been about to sacrifice the young girl.

"The Oki Islands are plagued by an evil sea god who demands the sacrifice of a young girl each year," he said. "If we disobey him, he becomes enraged. His storms cause the death of many of our fishermen. Thus we must sacrifice one to save the lives of many."

Tokoyo answered: "Pleases let me take her place. I have come to these islands to find my father who was banished by the emperor. I have not been able to reach him, and without him my life is empty. I have written a letter to him. If you would be so kind as to deliver it, I will die in peace."

Tokoyo knelt and prayed for courage. She put on the white robe the girl had worn, and she also placed her jeweled dagger between her teeth. While the girl and the priest watched, Tokoyo bowed low to them and then dived into the sea. Her body disappeared beneath the waves.

Tokoyo's years of diving gave her confidence. She descended deeper and deeper into the sea. As she reached the bottom she saw a huge cave covered with glittering shells. She took her dagger in her hand and swam into the cave, stopping quickly at the sight of a man. Looking more closely she realized it was a statue of the emperor who had banished her father. Working quickly, she removed the statue and began swimming back to the entrance of the cave.

Suddenly Tokoyo was startled by the sight of a huge scaly monster that had red eyes, many legs, and a long ridged tail. The beast was so big that it wallowed in the heavy sea. Having the advantage of speed, Tokoyo swam quickly forward and thrust her dagger into one eye. Pulling it out, she watched as the evil sea god floundered in the water, thrashing with pain, searching for refuge in its cave entrance. Wasting no time, Tokoyo swam forward again and stabbed the monster in the heart. In a matter of seconds, the creature drifted to the sea's floor, dying a painful death.

Tokoyo wanted to prove to the people of the island that they no longer needed to fear the sea god. Gasping with the last of her breath, she dragged the monster's body as she swam to the surface.

Only a few minutes had passed since Tokoyo had dived into the sea, so the priest and the young girl were still on the rocky cliffs above Tokoyo. Seeing her struggling with the statue and the body of the monster, they rushed down the rocks to help her. Once she had rested on the sand for a moment she told them of her brave adventure.

Tokoyo was then heralded by everyone on the island. Messengers were sent to the emperor whose health had miraculously improved. When he learned of the statue, he realized that an enemy had created his image, cursed it, and put it in the cave. By retrieving it, Tokoyo had broken the evil spell. The emperor wasted no time in releasing Oribe from his exile.

Tokoyo and her father were reunited, and they returned to their village and lands. Soon their lives were as before, and they rejoiced daily in their togetherness. The people of Oki never forgot the bravery of Tokoyo and tell of her feats even today.

The History of Whittington

(from *The Blue Fairy Book* edited by Andrew Lang)

Dick Whittington was a little boy when his father and mother died—so little that he never knew them—nor the place where he was born. He strolled about the country as ragged as a colt till he met with a wagoner who was going to London and who gave him leave to walk all the way by the side of his wagon without paying anything for his passage. This pleased little Whittington very much, as he sadly wanted to see London for he had heard that the streets were paved with gold, and he was willing to get a bushel of it. But how great was his disappointment—poor boy!—when he saw the streets covered with dirt instead of gold and found himself in a strange place without a friend, without food, and without money.

Though the wagoner was so charitable as to let him walk up by the side of the wagon for nothing, he took care not to know him when he came to town. The poor boy was, in a little time, so cold and so hungry that he wished himself in a good kitchen and by a warm fire in the country.

In this distress he asked charity of several people, and one of them bid him, "Go to work for an idle rogue."

"That I will," said Whittington, "with all my heart. I will work for you if you will let me."

The man, who thought this savored of wit and impertinence (though the poor lad intended only to show his readiness to work), gave him a blow with a stick that broke his head so that the blood ran down. In this situation, and fainting for want of food, he laid himself down at the door of one Mr. Fitzwarren, a merchant. There Mr. Fitzwarren's cook saw him, and being an ill-natured hussy, she ordered him to go about his business or she would scald him. At this time Mr. Fitzwarren came from the exchange and also began to scold the poor boy, bidding him to go to work.

Whittington answered that he should be glad to work if anybody would employ him and that he should be able if he could get some victuals to eat. He had had nothing for three days he said, and he was a poor country boy and knew nobody, and nobody would employ him.

He then endeavored to get up but was so weak that he fell down again, which excited so much compassion in the merchant that he ordered the servants to take him in and give him some meat and drink and let him help the cook to do any dirty work that she had. People are too apt to reproach those who beg with being idle. They do not concern themselves with putting them in the way of getting business to do or considering whether they are able to do it, which is not charity.

But we return to Whittington, who would have lived happily in this worthy family had he not been bumped about by the cross cook, who was always roasting or basting and who, when the spit was idle, employed her hands upon poor Whittington! At last Miss Alice, his master's daughter, was informed of it, and then she took compassion on the poor boy and made the servants treat him kindly.

Besides the crossness of the cook, Whittington had another difficulty to get over before he could be happy. He had, by order of his master, a flock bed placed for him in a garret, where there was a number of rats and mice that often ran over the poor boy's nose and disturbed him in his sleep. After some time, however, a gentleman who came to his master's house gave Whittington a penny for brushing his shoes. This he put into his pocket, being determined to lay it out to the best advantage. And the next day, seeing a woman in the street with a cat under her arm, he ran up to know the price of it. The woman (as the cat was a good mouser) asked a good deal of money for it, but on Whittington's telling her he had but a penny in the world and that he wanted a cat sadly, she let him have it.

This cat Whittington concealed in the garret, for fear she should be beat about by his mortal enemy the cook, and here she soon killed or frightened away the rats and mice so that the poor boy could then sleep as sound as a top.

Soon after this the merchant, who had a ship ready to sail, called for his servants, as his custom was, in order that each of them might venture something to try their luck. Whatever they sent was to pay neither freight nor custom, for he thought justly that God Almighty would bless him the more for his readiness to let the poor partake of his fortune.

All the servants appeared but poor Whittington, who, having neither money nor goods, could not think of sending anything to try his luck. But his good friend, Miss Alice, thinking his poverty kept him away, ordered him to be called.

She then offered to lay down something for him, but the merchant told his daughter that that would not do. It had to be something of his own. Upon which poor

Whittington said he had nothing but a cat that he had bought for a penny that was given him.

"Fetch thy cat, boy," said the merchant, "and send her."

Whittington took poor puss and delivered her to the captain with tears in his eyes, for he said he should now be disturbed by the rats and mice as much as ever. All the company laughed at the adventure, but Miss Alice, who pitied the poor boy, gave him something to buy another cat.

While puss was beating the billows at sea, poor Whittington was severely beaten at home by his tyrannical mistress the cook, who used him so cruelly and made such game of him for sending his cat to sea that at last the poor boy determined to run away from his place. Having packed up the few things he had, he set out very early in the morning on All Hallows day. He traveled as far as Holloway and there sat down on a stone to consider what course he should take. But while he was thus ruminating, Bow bells, of which there were only six, began to ring. He thought their sounds addressed him in this manner:

Turn again, Whittington,
Thrice Lord Mayor of London.

Lord Mayor of London! said he to himself. What would not one endure to be Lord Mayor of London and ride in such a fine coach? Well, I will go back again and bear all the pummeling and ill usage of Cicely rather than miss the opportunity of being Lord Mayor! So home he went and happily got into the house and about his business before Mrs. Cicely made her appearance.

We must now follow Miss Puss to the coast of Africa. How perilous are voyages at sea, how uncertain the winds and the waves, and how many accidents attend a naval life!

The ship that had the cat on board was long beaten at sea and at last, by contrary winds, driven on a part of the coast of Barbary that was inhabited by Moors unknown to the English. These people received our countrymen with civility, and therefore the captain, in order to trade with them, showed them the patterns of the goods he had on board and sent some of them to the king of the country, who was so well pleased that he sent for the captain and the factor to be brought to his palace, which was about a mile from the sea. Here they were placed, according to the custom of the country, on rich carpets flowered with gold and silver. And with the king and queen seated at the upper end of the room, dinner was brought in, which consisted of many dishes. But no sooner were the dishes put down than an amazing number of rats and mice came from all quarters and devoured all the meat in an instant.

The factor, in surprise, turned round to the nobles and asked if these vermin were not offensive. "Oh! yes," said they, "very offensive. The king would give half his treasure to be freed of them, for they not only destroy his dinner, as you see, but they assault him in his chamber—even in bed—so that he is obliged to be watched while he is sleeping for fear of them."

The factor jumped for joy. He remembered poor Whittington and his cat and told the king he had a creature on board the ship that would dispatch all these vermin immediately. The king's heart heaved so high at the joy this news gave him that his turban dropped off his head.

"Bring this creature to me," said he. "Vermin are dreadful in a court, and if she will perform what you say, I will load your ship with gold and jewels in exchange for her."

The factor, who knew his business, took this opportunity to set forth the merits of Miss Puss. He told his majesty that it would be inconvenient to part with her, as when she was gone, the rats and mice might destroy the goods in the ship—but to oblige his majesty he would fetch her.

"Run, run," said the queen. "I am impatient to see the dear creature."

Away flew the factor, while another dinner was being provided, and he returned with the cat just as the rats and mice were devouring that also. He immediately put down Miss Puss, who killed a great number of them.

The king rejoiced greatly to see his old enemies destroyed by so small a creature, and the queen was highly pleased and desired the cat might be brought near that she might look at her. Upon which the factor called "Pussy, pussy, pussy!" and she came to him. He then presented her to the queen, who started back and was afraid to touch a creature who had made such a havoc among the rats and mice. However, when the factor stroked the cat and called "Pussy, pussy!" the queen also touched her and cried "Putty, putty!" for she had not learned English.

He then put her down on the queen's lap, where she, purring, played with her majesty's hand and then sang herself to sleep.

The king, having seen the exploits of Miss Puss and being informed that her kittens would stock the whole country, bargained with the captain and factor for the whole ship's cargo and then gave them ten times as much for the cat as all the rest amounted to. On which, taking leave of their majesties and other great personages at court, they sailed with a fair wind for England, whither we must now attend them.

The morn had scarcely dawned when Mr. Fitzwarren arose to count over the cash and settle the business for that day. He had just entered the countinghouse and seated himself at the desk when somebody came tap, tap at the door.

"Who's there?" asked Mr. Fitzwarren.

"A friend," answered the other.

"What friend can come at this unseasonable time?"

"A real friend is never unseasonable," answered the other.

"I come to bring you good news of your ship *Unicorn*."

The merchant bustled up in such a hurry that he forgot his gout and instantly opened the door. Who should be seen waiting but the captain and factor, with a cabinet of jewels and a bill of lading, for which the merchant lifted up his eyes and thanked heaven for sending him such a prosperous voyage. Then they told him the adventures of the cat and showed him the cabinet of jewels that they had brought for Mr. Whittington. Upon which he cried out with great earnestness but not in the most poetical manner:

Go, send him in, and tell him of his fame,
And call him Mr. Whittington by name.

It is not our business to animadvert upon these lines—we are not critics but historians. It is sufficient for us that they are the words of Mr. Fitzwarren. And though it is beside our purpose and perhaps not in our power to prove him a good poet, we shall soon convince the reader that he was a good man, which was a much better character. For when some who were present told him that this treasure was too much for such a poor boy as Whittington, he said: "God forbid that I should deprive him of a penny. It is his own, and he shall have it to a farthing." He then ordered Mr. Whittington in, who was at this time cleaning the kitchen and would have excused himself from going into the countinghouse, saying the room was swept and his shoes were dirty and full of hobnails. The merchant, however, made him come in and ordered a chair to be set for him. Upon which, thinking they intended to make sport of him—as had been too often the case in the kitchen—he besought his master not to mock a poor simple fellow who intended them no harm but to let him go about his business. The merchant, taking him by the hand, said: "Indeed, Mr. Whittington, I am in earnest with you and sent for you to congratulate you on your great success.

Your cat has procured you more money than I am worth in the world, and may you long enjoy it and be happy!"

At length, being shown the treasure and convinced by them that all of it belonged to him, he fell upon his knees and thanked the Almighty for his providential care of such a poor and miserable creature. He then laid all the treasure at his master's feet, who refused to take any part of it but told him he heartily rejoiced at his prosperity and hoped the wealth he had acquired would be a comfort to him and would make him happy. He then applied to his mistress, and to his good friend Miss Alice, who refused to take any part of the money but who told him she heartily rejoiced at his good success and wished him all imaginable felicity. He then gratified the captain, factor, and the ship's crew for the care they had taken of his cargo. He likewise distributed presents to all the servants in the house, not forgetting even his old enemy the cook, though she little deserved it.

After this Mr. Fitzwarren advised Mr. Whittington to send for the necessary people and dress himself like a gentlemen, and he made him the offer of his house to live in till he could provide himself with a better.

Now it came to pass when Mr. Whittington's face was washed, his hair curled, and he was dressed in a rich suit of clothes that he turned out a genteel young fellow. And as wealth contributes much to give a man confidence, he in a little time dropped that sheepish behavior that was principally occasioned by a depression of spirits. He soon grew a sprightly and good companion, insomuch that Miss Alice, who had formerly pitied him, fell in love with him.

When her father perceived they had this good liking for each other, he proposed a match between them. Both parties cheerfully consented. The Lord Mayor, Court of Aldermen, Sheriffs, the Company of Stationers, the Royal Academy of Arts, and a number of eminent merchants attended the ceremony and were elegantly treated at an entertainment made for that purpose.

History further relates that they lived very happily, had several children, and died at a good old age. Mr. Whittington served Sheriff of London and was three times Lord Mayor. In the last year of his mayoralty he entertained King Henry V and his queen, after his conquest of France, upon which occasion the king, in consideration of Whittington's merit, said, "Never had prince such a subject," which being told to Whittington at the table he replied, "Never had subject such a king." His majesty, out of respect to his good character, conferred the honor of knighthood on him soon after.

Sir Richard many years before his death constantly fed a great number of poor citizens, built a church and a college to it, with a yearly allowance for poor scholars, and near it erected a hospital.

He also built Newgate for criminals and gave liberally to St. Bartholomew's Hospital and other public charities.

(Reprinted by permission of the publisher.)

The Star Money

(collected by Jacob Grimm and Wilhelm Grimm)

There was once a time when a little girl had both her father and mother die. She was so poor that she no longer had any little room to live in or bed to sleep in, and at last she had nothing else but the clothes she was wearing. To eat, she only had a little bit of bread in her hand that some charitable soul had given her. She was, however, both good and pious. Because she was forsaken by all the world, she ventured forth in the open country.

A poor man met her and said: "Ah, give me something to eat. I am so hungry!"

She handed him the whole piece of bread and gave him blessings. As she traveled she came to a child who moaned: "My head is so cold. Give me something to cover it with!"

The little girl took off her hood and gave it to the child. When she had walked a little farther, she met another child who had no jacket and was frozen with cold. She gave that child her own coat to end his shivering. A little farther on, yet another child begged for a frock, so she gave hers away also. At length she came into a forest, and it had already become dark. What should she see but another child who asked for a little shirt. The good little girl thought to herself: It is a dark night, and no one sees you. You can very easily give your little shirt away. So she took it off and gave it to the child.

She then had not one single thing left. Suddenly some stars from heaven fell down, and they were nothing else but hard, smooth pieces of money. Even though she had just given her little shirt away, she had a new one of the very finest linen. She gathered together the money, put it into the shirt, and was rich all the days of her life.

Discussion

Around the world folktales such as these are concerned with the loss of a parent. In many cases, life was hard for the children. Not only was there Hansel and Gretel, Tokoyo, Dick, and the little girl, but also Cinderella, Snow White and Rose Red, and Snow White and the seven dwarfs, and Jack and the beanstalk. Diane Wolkstein includes a dead-mother story, "The Singing Bone," in her *The Magic Orange Tree and Other Haitian Folktales*. Many African stories also use this theme. We must stop and address here the stereotype of the stepmother that is created by these stories. Yes, stepmothers of today are not like the stepmothers of folktales who killed the first wife's children. Of course, it would not be fair to carry this perception further. However, in folktales, which were abbreviated forms of teaching what was right and what was wrong, how to live the good life, what behavior would be rewarded and what would be punished, step-mothers and stepfathers were generally there due to the death of the parent. And, of course, these stories were full of layers of teaching of morals and law. The message was clear: Take the role of stepmother or stepfather (or parent) seriously, and be as fair as possible to all of the children in the family. Consider as well the ancient times in which these stories were told and formed. Many parents died early because of childbirth complications, lack of today's medical techniques and medicines, bad diets, and a world full of disease and danger. These conditions made these stories part of the everyday life in which parents sometimes died or disappeared.

There are many other books and stories that deal with the loss of a parent. Joan Lowery Nixon has written a quartet of books based on the orphan trains of the 1800s in our country. The orphan trains were part of a program to give homeless children of New York City a chance for better and happier lives. In the mid-1800s when the entire population of New York City was around 500,000, the police estimated that there were 10,000 homeless children wandering the streets. Some of the children were orphans, some had been thrown out of their homes by parents. This was occurring at about the same time that Charles Dickens was writing his stories of the street children in London. Times were hard, conditions were desperate, and life was horrible.

Children were placed on trains that traveled to rural western destinations. Ads had been placed at places of the trains' arrival, and people would go to view the children. Hopefully the children would be adopted and find a better life. From 1854 to 1929 the Children's Aid Society sent more than 10,000 children on orphan trains from the slums of New York City to new homes in the West.

It is not only the loss of parents that children suffer. Beloved grandparents, friends, and pets become part of children's grieving. Therefore, the bibliography deals broadly with losses of several kinds as well as cites books that touch on death in general.

Fear of losing a parent is closely linked to another of the recorded fears of children. That is, of course, family fights. In both of these categories there is a deep sense of hopelessness, and family fights are interpreted by the listening children as future loss of parents. Divorce and the separation of the parents clearly represent this loss.

Activities

- Describe the characters in Hansel and Gretel or Dick Whittington. What did you think of them? How did they show whether they were cruel or kind, selfish or unselfish? Where some of the characters both cruel and kind? Had any of the characters grown and developed as a result of what they experienced? If so, who and how?

- Discuss Tokoyo's bravery and devotion. Can students think of other stories with a similar theme? Have students watch the newspapers for true-life examples.

- Browse through collections of folk stories from throughout the world, and see how many stories you can find that include stepmothers and stepfathers. Keep card files of the stories, references, and some information about them.

- Have you ever lost someone who was very special to you? Tell about it.

- Have you ever lost a pet that you loved? Share your story. You might illustrate a written story about this pet.

Bibliography

Babbit, Natalie. *Tuck Everlasting.* New York: Farrar, Straus and Giroux, 1975.
   This is a story about immortality and death. A girl of 10 meets a family that has drunk at a spring that has given them eternal life. Babbit wrote this after her own mother died and she raged: "Why her? She was needed." Then she began to consider the possibility of some people living forever and what the burdens of immortality are.

Barchers, Suzanne I. "The Tale of the Oki Islands." In *Wise Women: Folk and Fairy Tales from Around the World*, 13-15. Englewood, Colo.: Libraries Unlimited, 1990.
   A brave daughter rescues her banished father, restores the emperor to health, and vanquishes the evil sea god.

Bauer, Marion Dane. *On My Honor.* New York: Clarion, 1986.
   When his best friend drowns while they are swimming in a treacherous river that they had promised never to go near, Joel is devastated and terrified at having to tell both sets of parents the terrible consequences of their disobedience.

Bunting, Eve. *The Happy Funeral.* New York: Harper & Row, 1982.
   A little Chinese-American girl pays tribute to her grandfather as she assists in the preparations for his funeral.

Clifton, Lucille. *Everett Anderson's Goodbye.* New York: Holt, Rinehart and Winston, 1983.
   Everett Anderson has a difficult time coming to terms with his grief after his father dies. He goes through the five stages of grieving.

MacLachlan, Patricia. *Sarah, Plain and Tall.* New York: Harper & Row, 1985.
   After their mother has died, children react to their father's new mail-order bride. Life in Wyoming with her new family is a real adjustment for Sarah.

Miles, Miska. *Annie and the Old One.* Boston: Little, Brown, 1971.
   Annie cannot imagine her world without the Old One, her grandmother. The Old One has announced that she will go to Mother Earth when the new rug she is working on is taken from the loom. Annie refuses to accept this.

Munsch, Robert. *Love You Forever.* Scarborough, Ontario: Firefly Books, 1986.
   A young mother holds her child and sings him a love song. The story takes that baby through the stages of childhood until he becomes a man. The book is dedicated to the two stillborn babies of the Munschs'.

Nixon, Joan Lowery. *The Orphan Train Quartet: A Family Apart,* 1987; *In the Face of Danger,* 1988; *Caught in the Act,* 1988; and *A Place to Belong,* 1989. All published by Bantam.
   An immigrant family from Ireland try to escape the famine in their country but are not able to do much better in America. The father becomes ill and dies. The oldest of the four children gets in trouble with the law, and the mother sends her children to new lives by way of the orphan train in an effort to keep them from being sent to jail with adult criminals. This is the imagined story of their lives.

Paterson, Katherine. *Bridge to Terabithia.* New York: Thomas Y. Crowell, 1977.
   Two youngsters—a boy and a girl—are best friends. She dies in an accident, and the young boy comes to realize that he has not completely lost her. A powerful story of friendship and death.

Ross, Lillian. *The Little Old Man and His Dreams.* New York: Harper & Row, 1990.
   God comes to an old man in his dreams and allows him to attend his granddaughter's wedding. But in return the old man must go to live with God.

Thomas, Jane Resh. *Saying Good-Bye to Grandma.* New York: Clarion, 1988.
   Seven-year-old Suzie is curious and fearful about what Grandma's funeral will be like.

Tompert, Ann. *Will You Come Back for Me?* Illustrations by Robin Kramer. Niles, Ill.: Albert Whitman, 1988.
   Four-year-old Suki is worried about being left in day care for the first time until her mother reassures her that she loves her and will always return for her.

Varley, Susan. *Badger's Parting Gifts.* New York: Lothrop, Lee & Shepard, 1984.

Badger's friends are sad when he dies, but they treasure the legacies he left them. Everyone who knew him has warm and loving memories of when he was living. Through these memories Badger becomes part of their lives once more.

Viorst, Judith. *The Good-Bye Book.* Illustrations by Kay Chorao. New York: Atheneum, 1988.

On the verge of being left behind by parents who are going out for the evening, a child comes up with a variety of pleas and excuses to try and keep them home. Another look at separation anxiety and fears of abandonment.

____. *The Tenth Good Thing About Barney.* Illustrations by Erik Blegvad. New York: Atheneum, 1971.

With the death of their beloved pet, mother asks the children to be ready to say 10 good things about Barney as they say good-bye to him and bury him.

Wolkstein, Diane. "The Singing Bone." In *The Magic Orange Tree and Other Haitian Folktales*, 92-97. Illustrations by Elsa Henriquez. New York: Knopf, 1978.

The singing bone of the dead mother catches the guilty killer.

Zolotow, Charlotte. *A Father Like That.* New York: Harper & Row, 1971.

A young son who has never seen his father tells his mother what it would be like if his father were there. After she listens, she tells him to remember all those things so that he can be that kind of father some day.

____. *My Grandson Lew.* New York: Harper & Row, 1974.

Lew misses his grandfather, even though he died when Lew was two years old. A warm, rich, comforting book about sharing memories of someone.

The Two Travelers
(collected by Jacob Grimm and Wilhelm Grimm)

A shoemaker and a tailor crossed paths during their travels. The tailor was a pleasant, good-looking fellow, and the shoemaker was rather gruff and sour. They decided to become traveling companions and head for the big cities where they could find work.

When they got to a city, the tailor always managed to get some work. The sullen shoemaker never met with much success. The tailor happily shared with his companion and gaily spent what money he had. Their travels took them to the edge of a great forest that had two paths through it. One path took seven days and the other two, but they did not know which path was the short one. The shoemaker decided to carry bread enough for seven days of travel, but the tailor decided to only plan on two days of food. He felt sure they would find the right path, and he did not want to be burdened with perishable food. After traveling two days the tailor had eaten all of his provisions. The shoemaker, though, showed no mercy for the tailor. Each day he refused to share his food. On the fifth day the tailor was exhausted and weak. The shoemaker said, "I'll give you a piece of bread, but in return I'm going to cut out your right eye." The tailor's food cost him dearly that day.

On the sixth day the tailor was near death from hunger and made the same bargain with the shoemaker. He realized that he had been leading a very frivolous life, and when blind he could no longer earn a living sewing, but would have to become a beggar. He pleaded with the shoemaker to take him with him when he was blind. The shoemaker finished the bargain and gave the blind tailor a stick to use. They came out of the forest at sunset. There before them was a gallows standing in the field. The shoemaker left the blind tailor there and went on his way.

There were two men hanging from the gallows. One of the dead men spoke to the tailor. He told him that if he washed in the dew, he would regain his sight. The tailor did as he was told, and his vision returned. He saw the distant city and took off for it. In a field he saw a brown foal and caught it by its mane and intended to ride it into the city. The foal argued that he was too young and weak to be ridden and begged the tailor to let him remain free. And so the tailor let him go.

The hungry tailor traveled on and vowed to eat the next thing to cross his path. A stork came along, and the tailor caught it. The stork pleaded for his life, saying that he was a sacred bird. He also promised to repay the tailor if he would only free him. The tailor could not refuse the story. The city was still quite a distance away and hunger was growing keener. Again the tailor vowed to eat whatever he came upon. This time he came across two ducks swimming in a pond. Before he could wring the neck of one of the ducks, the old mother duck swam up and implored him to have mercy. She convinced the tailor to spare her babies.

Next, the tailor saw wild bees in a tree and decided to gather the honey for food. The queen bee threatened to sting him to death and begged for the tailor to leave the bees and the nest alone. Again, the kindly tailor agreed, and the queen bee promised to help him in return some day. The tailor crawled into the city to an inn where he finally ate. Revived, he looked for work and a place to stay. Things improved for him until at last he was appointed to be the king's tailor.

What a surprise it was for him to find out that on that same day the shoemaker became the court shoemaker. The shoemaker, fearing vengeance, plotted to turn the king against the tailor. He claimed that the tailor had boasted that he could recover the golden crown that had been lost for hundreds of years. The king ordered the tailor to do just that or else leave the city forever.

The tailor decided there was nothing for him to do but to leave the city, so he packed his knapsack. When he arrived at the pond where he had met the ducks, the mother duck told him not to worry. She and her 12 ducklings dived down into the water and swam back to him with the magnificent crown. The king rewarded him when he returned the crown, but the shoemaker again plotted to get rid of him. This time he told the king that the tailor was boasting again about how he could make a wax model of the entire royal palace with everything in it.

Again the king summoned the tailor and demanded he build the model. Failure to do so would be punished with life imprisonment in an underground dungeon. The tailor packed his knapsack and left. When he got to the hollow tree, he sat down to rest and think. The queen bee asked him what was wrong, and after he told her she instructed him to return the next day with a large cloth. The bees flew into the castle and explored it thoroughly and built an exact replica of wax. The surprised king put this amazing model on display.

The shoemaker was not daunted. He again returned to the king and whispered to him that the tailor was bragging that he could make water gush in the middle of the courtyard. The king again summoned the tailor and demanded him to make good the boast or else he would lose his head. The troubled tailor left the city for the third time and returned to the foal, who by this time had grown up. The horse told him to climb on his back, and they galloped straight into the courtyard, where the horse sped around the yard three times. The third time the horse crashed to the ground and a piece of earth in the middle of the courtyard erupted with a gush of crystal clear water. The pleased king embraced the tailor in front of everyone in the court.

The wicked shoemaker would not give up, however. This time he told the king that the tailor was arrogantly boasting that he could have a son brought through the air. The king had plenty of daughters but no sons. He promised to reward the tailor with his oldest daughter in marriage if he could do such a thing within nine days. The tailor decided that he could never live in peace in the king's kingdom, so he once more packed up and rushed away. This time he came upon the stork, who promised to help him out of this predicament. The stork told him to be at the palace within nine days, and sure enough the stork put a lovely baby boy into the outstretched arms of the queen.

His good fortune prompted the tailor to remember his mother's advice to be good and that with a little bit of luck he would find happiness. As for the troublemaking shoemaker, before being banished from the kingdom by the king he had to make the shoes for the tailor to dance in at his own wedding. And justice was truly served when the shoemaker found himself below the gallows. He threw himself down on the ground to rest and closed his eyes. With that, two crows on the heads of each of the hanging dead men flew down and pecked out the shoemaker's eyes. He disappeared into the forest and was never seen of or heard from again.

Discussion

Blindness has often been the result of physical and public health conditions. Delay in detection and correction of certain situations will result in blindness. But according to Kaoru Yamamoto in a *Journal of Child Psychology and Psychiatry* article: "There is the deep fear, and the attendant stigma, of blindness in Egypt where children often curse each other by saying, 'I hope God makes you blind!' Blind people are seen to be worthless, weak, unkind, passive, dirty and slow." For aeons, blindness has been viewed as a form of punishment. In the Bible this passage from Exodus (21:23-26) is found: "And if any mischief follow then thou shalt give life for life, eye for eye, tooth for tooth, hand for hand, foot for foot, burning for burning, wound for wound, stripe for stripe. And if a man smite the eye of his servant, or the eye of his maid, that it perish; he shall let him go free for his eye's sake." Also in the Bible in a passage from Judges (16:19-20), Sampson is blinded by the Philistines after Delilah cuts his hair.

Other evidence of blinding as punishment is found in early cultures in dealing with criminals. Either one or both eyes were put out and this was certainly a symbol of death. Mythology also contains instances of blinding not only as punishment but as a consequence of revenge, reprisal, ambition, or jealousy. Orion and Oedipus were both punished by blinding. In Matthew 5:29 Jesus says, "And if thy right eye offend thee, pluck it out, and cast it from thee for it is profitable for thee that one of thy members should perish, and not that thy whole body should be cast into hell." The Grimms' version of Cinderella finds the two stepsisters being blinded by two pigeons during the wedding procession because of their greed and unkindness.

In current times blindness as punishment is still a threat. Many times as a child caught reading in bed under the blankets with a flashlight, I was told that I would go blind. Boys are threatened with blindness as a punishment for masturbation. Back in the early 1960s I worked with a six-year-old child who was immobilized by the fear of going blind. After talking with her and her family we discovered that the parents had repeatedly threatened the girl with blindness if she should ever take drugs. These threats were made concrete by a well-publicized case of some young men who, while under the influence of drugs, lay down and looked at the sun and became blind.

Many idioms exist in our language that are related to blindness. For example, an expression of contempt is to be referred to as one-eyed. Blindness can also be involved in trickery. In Genesis 27, for example, Jacob tricks his blind father, Isaac, and gains the blessing intended for his brother Esau. Jewish folk stories also touch on blindness being used for trickery. One story tells of a blind beggar with a tin cup piteously seeking money. An old Jewish woman gives him a dime, and the beggar is filled with joy. "As soon as I took the first look at you I knew you had a kind heart" is the beggar's remark.

All these extremely negative connotations concerning blindness should be countered with a less threatening aspect and placed into the category of being a genuine misfortune and not a punishment. Losing one's sight is a possible condition of life.

Activities

- Guide children to an understanding and empathy for anyone who is blind. Children can be blindfolded and led around familiar surroundings. What do they hear, smell, feel? This can be extended to unfamiliar surroundings. Afterward, children can discuss how someone who is blind might feel and think.

- Read stories about people such as Helen Keller who have triumphed over blindness.

- What people have achieved success in the arts who are blind?

- Invite people who have lost their eyesight to discuss and share their feelings and thoughts. People who have been blind from birth might have different reactions. Why?

- Invite an eye doctor to class to answer questions and share experiences.

- Enos Mills, one of the first environmentalists and the founding father of Rocky Mountain National Park, wrote of the experience of being snow-blind while climbing Longs Peak on the continental divide in Colorado. Read or listen to the story "Blind on the Continental Divide," and list the ways Enos compensated for his blindness as he struggled to survive.

Bibliography

Adler, David A. *The Helen Keller Story.* Illustrations by John Wallner and Alexandra Wallner. New York: Holiday House, 1990.
    A biography of the woman who overcame her handicaps of being blind and deaf.

DeArmond, Dale. *The Seal Oil Lamp: Adapted from an Eskimo Folktale.* Boston: Sierra Club, distributed by Little, Brown, 1988.
    Allugua, who was born blind, is saved from death when Mouse Woman repays the boy for an earlier kindness to her baby mouse. The strong wood engravings are a nice balance to this powerful story.

Fisher, Leonard Everett. *Cyclops.* New York: Holiday House, 1991.
    Fisher, through words and illustrations, describes the encounter between the Cyclops Polyphemus, and Odysseus and his men after the end of the Trojan War.

Martin, Bill, Jr., and John Archambault. Illustrations by Ted Rand. *Knots on a Counting Rope.* New York: Henry Holt, 1987.
    This is the poignant story of the special relationship between a blind Indian boy and his grandfather who uses a counting rope to help the youngster face the many challenges of life. The counting rope is a metaphor for the passage of time and for the boy's emerging confidence. Truly a beautiful book in art and message.

Randall, Glenn. "Blind on the Continental Divide." *Longs Peak Tales*. Self-published. Denver, Colo., 1981.

Enos Mills climbed Longs Peak many times during his life. One time, though, he forgot sunglasses and went snow-blind. This is the story of how he kept his wits about him and found his way back down the mountain. The story is filled with observations of what Mills "saw" through his senses to help him survive.

Steptoe, John. *The Story of Jumping Mouse*. New York: Lothrop, Lee & Shepard, 1984.

The smallest and humblest of creatures can dream of courage if the creature is faithful to itself and its dream. This story of the Plains Indians is told and illustrated with compassion and power.

Storm, Hyemeyohsts. *Seven Arrows*. New York: Ballantine, 1972.

Many old stories of the Plains Indian tribes are told in *Seven Arrows*. These stories were used to teach the meanings of the Sun Dance Way. From beginning to end, the book is a teaching story. The story of Jumping Mouse can be found on pages 68 to 85.

Taylor, Theodore. *The Cay*. New York: Doubleday, 1969.

A young boy and his mother are on a ship torpedoed by a German submarine in the Caribbean during World War II. The boy, Philip, finds himself alone on a raft with an old black man, Timothy. Philip goes blind as a delayed result of the shipwreck injury. Before he dies, Timothy teaches Philip to fend for himself as well as some lessons about love and respect.

Yolen, Jane. *The Seeing Stick*. Illustrations by Remy Charlip and Demetra Maraslis. New York: Thomas Y. Crowell, 1977.

An old man teaches the Chinese emperor's blind daughter to see. The ending of the story is a striking surprise. Yolen writes literary folk stories with imagination and skill.

Reference

Yamamoto, Kaoru, Abdalla Soliman, James Parsons, and O. L. Davies, Jr. "Voices in Unison: Stressful Events in the Lives of Children in Six Countries." *Journal of Child Psychology and Psychiatry* 28, no. 6 (1987): 855-64.

The Town Where No One Might Urinate
(from Africa)

> *Cook my sweetmeats,*
> *Cook them tender,*
> *Cook good things,*
> *My daughter will remember.*

The mother was anxiously preparing for a visit with her daughter who lived in a town where no one was allowed to urinate. She sang this rhyme as she cooked and packed for the trip. When all was done and she was sure she had made enough of her daughter's favorite foods, she took off.

Her son-in-law was the first to greet her. "My mother-in-law has come," he said. "Welcome! Welcome!" To show her how special her visit was, he killed a chicken and also fixed some rice for her.

"Mother, it is so good to have you here," said the daughter. "Just please, please remember not to eat or drink too much. You know that no one in this town is allowed to urinate."

"Dear daughter, thank you for that information! I knew that before you were born," snorted the mother.

The daughter knew that nothing she said would matter, so she paid no more attention to her mother's eating and drinking. Did that mother listen to her daughter? After all, she had been on a long, hot journey, and she knew how to live her own life, did she not? And so she ate until she was full and drank until her thirst was quenched.

They went to bed, and in the middle of the night the mother was quite uncomfortable. What can I do? she thought. I really need to go. But where can I possibly do it without being caught? She did everything she could think of to avoid thinking about urinating. Finally she could take it no longer. She quietly got up and went to where the horses were kept. "No one will find out if I go here!" she said triumphantly. With great relief she urinated and then covered the place with some cut grass.

It was not to happen that easily, however. The earth was not used to what she had done, and the very part of the earth where she had urinated rose up and began to complain.

Umm, umm, I am not used to this,
Umm, umm, I am not used to this.

This woke all the people, and they came to where the earth was moaning. "Who has urinated here? Who has done this thing?" they all cried. "Bring out the magic gourds. Let everyone come here and step over the small gourd and then the large gourd. The gourds will catch hold of the person who has broken the law and urinated." And so it was done.

The two magic gourds were carefully carried out and placed on the ground. Everyone in the village, one by one, stepped over the gourds. What a surprise! The gourds did not move. They did not jump up and seize anyone. The people all puzzled over this until one of them remembered something and said: "There is a stranger in our village. Have the visitor come and step over the gourds."

When the mother came and saw the people and the two magic gourds, she immediately started to shake. She was shaking so much that it was hard for her to lift her leg up to step over the gourds, and as she stood above them shaking and unsteady, they jumped up and grabbed her. "She is the one. She is the one who has urinated," everyone cried.

The gourds began to sing:

Mother-in-law has done it,
We have seized her tight,
Mother-in-law has done it,
What a guilty sight.

Poor mother-in-law. She jumped and hopped around. She stamped and stomped and tried to shake them off but the gourds hung on. She could not even sit down or she would be sitting on them. Was life to be this way forever?

Spider, that interfering character, happened by and saw her and watched her and exclaimed: "Oh, you lucky mother-in-law! You have gourds on you that sing a very beautiful song. How very lucky you are. Oh, I should like to have them. Please let me try them on!"

Mother-in-law whispered to the spider: "Very well. I will share with you. But first you have to urinate on the ground, and then when anyone asks who did that, all you have to say is that it was not you, it was not you, it was not you who did it."

And so the spider did as he had been told. "There!" he said. "I did not do it. I did not do it. I did not do it! Come magic gourds to me. I admire your songs and want to dance to them." As soon as the spider said this, the gourds let go of the woman and seized him. They changed their song.

The things which clasp and hold tight,
Have caught spider of spider this very night.

How pleased the spider was. He began to dance to the music of the gourds. What fun! After a while though, he became tired and said: "Mother-in-law, do not feel slighted. Come and take your gourds. Thank you for sharing them with me."

Mother-in-law refused to take them back. Spider began to plead with her, but mother-in-law just watched and moved away from him. Spider went into a frenzy to try to shake the gourds off. Finally, he climbed a tall tree. When at the very top, he threw himself down to the ground—buttocks first—to smash the gourds and get free. They only moved to one side of him and were not broken in the fall, but the spider's back was broken, and he died. With that, the magic gourds returned to where they had come from. When they were gone, all the villagers began to urinate. There was no more harm to anyone for urinating.

Discussion

The fear of urinating was a problem for everyone in this village. And as the story proves, children are not the only ones who worry about such accidents in life. It would seem that adults do too.

A secret education of children is at work throughout the world. Subjects that are taboo nevertheless become part of the lore and language and games of children. This secret knowledge is passed on through generations by rhyme, jump-rope chants, and verses. Consider the following rhymes collected by folklorists.

Fatty, Fatty, two-by-four,
Couldn't get through the bathroom door,
So he did it on the floor.

Red, Red, wet your bed.
(directed at redheads)

What made Miss Tomato turn red?
She saw Mr. Green pea.

King of France wet his pants
Right in the middle of a wedding dance.
How many puddles did he make?

How dry I am, how wet I'll be,
If I don't find the bathroom key.
I found the key, now where's the door—
Oops, too late, it's on the floor.

Whenever you ask children to share their secret rhymes with you, their eyes grow big, and at first they refuse. They are only protecting us adults from the shocking things of the world. These forbidden bits of bathroom lore are part of a ritualistic rebellion and give children a kind of prestige among their peers. It is all part of the lore and language learning of childhood. It also helps reinforce existing social taboos.

Why are these verses remembered half a century later? Is it the forbidden-fruit syndrome? Can you remember the trick at camp or at overnight parties where someone gets a pan of warm water and places the hand of a sleeping friend in it? Remember that? Why? It is all part of that social taboo and flying in the face of fear. We all fear such a social calamity. For children, the fear of an accident in school is real. Children have to ask permission to go to the bathroom, and sometimes they can forget and wait too long to ask. The cruel teasing by other children—grateful that it did not happen to them—follows them for days. The fear of wetting in class is a real fear children live with.

Comic strips deal with this topic easily today. In a recent Mother Goose and Grimm strip, Grimm is being pushed into a corner by a rabid, drooling, fanged dog. Grimm says, "Some dogs can sense if you're frightened." In the next frame Grimm adds, "I wonder if he can sense that I just piddled down my leg?" And the grouchiest of all school-bus drivers, Crankshaft, comments: "I asked you if anyone had to go before we left! Sometimes I wonder if driving the football team is worth the extra pay!"

Activities

- Recite some rhymes from your childhood. Ask the children to share some they know. You will probably be surprised. My four-year-old granddaughter already knows some.

- Discuss the fear of wetting your pants while in school.

- Discuss how fear itself can lead to these accidents.

- "I laughed so hard I peed in my pants." This statement is a common one. Discuss why this can be a problem.

- Does your family have a ritual saying before leaving on a trip?— "Everyone go potty!" Why is this? Have you ever suffered while traveling until you reached the next pit stop?

- Read and share the books by Robert Munsch and Anna Ross with children. Can they remember a time in their lives when similar things took place as occur in these stories?

Bibliography

Knapp, May, and Herbert Knapp. *One Potato, Two Potato ...* New York: Norton, 1976.
   The play of children in jokes, jeers, clapping games, riddles, jump-rope rhymes, and parodies is the secret education of children growing up.

Miller, Virginia. *On Your Potty!* New York: Greenwillow, 1991.
   Young bear Bartholomew finds that using his potty correctly is sometimes just a matter of the right timing.

Munsch, Robert. *I Have to Go.* Illustrations by Michael Martchenko. Toronto: Annick Press, 1989.
   Anyone who has ever lived with a little kid will recognize the situations in this book: the bundling up in the snowsuit, the trip, and the fateful accident in a strange bed.

Opie, Iona, and Peter Opie. *The Lore and Language of Schoolchildren.* London: Oxford University Press, 1959.
   The strange and primitive culture of modern out-of-school children is all here. It is based on information collected from 5,000 children in England.

Ross, Anna. *I Have to Go.* Illustrations by Norman Gorbaty. New York: Random House, 1990.
   The story features Jim Henson's Sesame Street Muppets and tells of how Little Grover goes to the bathroom all by himself—a milestone!

Ross, Tony. *I Want My Potty.* Brooklyn, N.Y.: Kane/Miller, 1988.
   A little princess—tired of diapers—learns to use the potty, although it is not always easy.

The Ugly Duckling

(by Hans Christian Andersen)

All the fields and meadows were full of summer's beauty and richness of crops. In the middle of it all were some deep lakes. In one of the lakes sat a mother duck on her nest. She had to hatch her eggs, but something was quite unusual. Among all the eggs was one that was quite different from the others. It was so big!

The mother duck sat and sat and sat on her eggs. It was really quite lonely doing that. The father of the ducks never came to visit her or to help her with the sitting on the eggs. An old duck came swimming by the nest and passed the time of day with mother duck.

"It's such a lovely day, mother duck. When are your babies going to come out and enjoy it all?" the old duck asked.

Mother duck just stood up and flapped her wings for some exercise as well as to dry them off. "I hope it is quite soon," she replied.

"What is that funny egg in your nest?" asked the old duck. "It looks like a turkey egg. I know because I was fooled by a turkey egg once. No matter what I did, it was afraid of the water and would not learn to quack and was a great nuisance."

"Oh," replied the mother duck as she settled back on her nest, "I do not think any turkey would have been able to fool me. I have been sitting on these eggs steady."

Old duck wagged its tail good-bye and swam off.

Finally a few days later, mother duck felt the little baby ducks breaking through their shells. They all hatched except for the large different egg. "I think I'll give it a few more days to hatch," mother duck said. Meanwhile, her babies were quacking and swimming around the nest. Finally the last egg burst, and the duck that emerged was ugly! It was large and did not look like any duck baby she had ever seen before. It surely was not a turkey, however, because it swam. With a mother's pride, she quickly decided that it really was not ugly but beautiful in a different way. And so they all went out to see the world.

Other ducks swam over to her family and pecked at her large baby. "It is peculiar and needs to go," said one of the ducks. Other ducks would fly by and bite it on its neck.

Mother duck was very protective of her baby. "Don't do that," she squawked, "Do you see what a pleasant disposition my baby has?"

Things only got worse as the other ducklings bit, pushed, and taunted her unusual baby. "It is big and does not belong here with us," one of the ducklings said. Even the little girl who came to the lake with corn and bread to feed the ducks kicked at it whenever it came to her for food. Finally the duckling swam off to hide in the reeds.

Two wild geese glided over to it, and one of them looked at the duckling with respect and said: "Hey, you are so ugly I like you. Why not fly away with us?" Just as they were taking off there were two loud noises, and both of the geese fell back into the water. There were hunters all around the lake shooting the birds. A big black dog jumped into the lake and started to swim out to the duckling, who closed his eyes and was ready to be eaten. But the dog just swam past him and seized the body of one of the geese that had fallen.

"I am so ugly that even the dog will not eat me," said the duckling. With that the duckling just lay quiet in the reeds. That evening it left the lake and ran through a booming storm. It ended up in a peasant's hut. The door was just hanging on one hinge, and the whole building was tilted to one side and about to fall over. Even so, inside was a woman with her pets. The next day when the woman saw the duckling, she had it join her household—only because she was thinking of what a delicious meal it would make when it was fattened up. The other animals, as seemed to always happen, expected the duckling to purr, lay eggs, have sensible opinions, and be clever. When it obviously did not do any of these things, the animals in the hut became disagreeable.

Once again, the duckling went to the water, swam, and dived but always was slighted by every creature because of its ugliness. By now it was autumn, and the trees in the forest turned yellow, red, and brown. The winds blew the leaves in straight lines into the forest. There was the sound of the crunch of leaves as animals traveled over them as well as a smell of rotting leaves. Dark clouds appeared, and with them came cold, damp air. Rain fell, and then it turned to snow. The duckling saw amazing things as flocks of birds flew in and swam for a while before taking off again. One special flock was sparkling white, with long graceful necks, and they flew away with glorious great wings. Oh, how the duckling loved seeing those happy, beautiful birds.

The winter was a harsh one. The duckling had to keep swimming to keep the lake's surface from freezing solid. In spite of it, though, each night the hole left in the ice kept getting smaller and smaller. The duckling used its legs and did everything possible to prevent the hole from freezing over, but at last he was too tired and froze into the ice.

In the morning a farmer walked by and saw the duckling. He took a stick and broke the ice away from the duckling and carried the duckling home to his wife. But things did not go much better there. The duckling became frightened by the children who wanted to play with it, and it flew, flapped, and fell in a frenzy, knocking things over and creating havoc. He escaped out the door and spent the rest of the winter in misery and sorrow. But, as always, spring came, and it was beautiful. The sun warmed the duckling, and he was able to flap his wings and beat the air. In fact, he flew and ended up in a thicket that looked inviting. To his amazement, three glorious white swans swam over to him. When he saw them, he prepared to fly away to save himself, because surely these splendid creatures would not want the likes of his ugliness around them. He changed his mind, though, and decided that maybe the best thing would be to let these royal birds kill him and settle everything forever. As he swam to them he bent his head down and saw something in the clear water that made him stop and stare. It was his reflection. He was a swan! His life was then quite different. All the swans accepted him, and the children who went to the water cried: "Look, there is a new one. He is the most beautiful of them all."

As he heard them making up songs about his beauty, he rejoiced from the depths of his heart. I am a swan. I am a beautiful swan, he thought. The ugly duckling is gone!

Clever Else

(collected by Jacob Grimm and Wilhelm Grimm)

There once was a man who had a daughter called Clever Else. When she was grown up, her father declared that she must get married, and, of course, Clever Else's mother agreed. In fact, the mother's only worry was that "we need to find someone whom Clever Else will consent to have."

After a long time a lad named Hans proposed to Clever Else—but only on the condition that she be careful as well as clever. "Have no fear," said Clever Else's father, "she does not want for brains at all."

"That is all fine and good that she is bright," said Hans, "but I insist that she be careful too."

They were all seated at the table and had eaten a substantial meal that Clever Else's mother had prepared. Because everyone was mellow from the food, the mother thought some beer would top the pleasant meal off, so she asked Else to go into the cellar and draw some beer.

Clever Else took the jug down from the hook on the wall, and as she went down to the cellar she rattled the jug lid up and down to help pass the time. Down in the cellar Else took a stool and placed it in front of the beer cask so that she would not need to stoop and get a sore back. She put the jug under the tap and turned it on. While the beer was running, she glanced around—again just to keep busy. She caught sight of a pickax that the workmen had left sticking in the ceiling just above her head. Clever Else thought, "If I marry Hans and we have a child and it grows big and we send it into the cellar to draw beer, that pickax might fall on its head and kill it." She began to cry with all of her might about the anticipated tragedy.

Meanwhile, everyone was waiting upstairs for something to drink. After a long while Else's mother asked the maid to "go down to the cellar and see why Else does not come back."

The maid found Else sitting in front of the cask crying and sobbing. "Why are you crying?" asked the maid.

"What else can I do except cry," answered Else. "If I marry Hans and we have a child and it grows big and we send it here to draw beer, perhaps the pickax may fall on its head and kill it."

"Our Else is indeed clever," commented the maid, and she sat down on the floor beside Else and began to sob herself.

When the maid did not return, the people upstairs became more and more thirsty and Else's father told the serving boy: "Go down to the cellar and see what Else and the maid are doing. I am getting very thirsty!"

The boy found both Clever Else and the maid sitting and crying together. "What is the matter?" he asked them.

"What else can we do except cry?" replied Else. "If I marry Hans and we have a child and it grows big and we send it here to draw beer, the pickax might fall on its head and kill it."

"Our Else is truly clever!" said the boy, and he sat down on the floor beside her and the maid and began howling himself.

And still the others waited upstairs. When the boy did not return, Else's father said to his wife, "Wife, you go down there to see what is going on."

Else's mother went down to the cellar and found the three bawling and spilling great tears. "What is going on here?" she cried above their uproar.

Else told her how the future possible child might be killed by the pickax falling on its head when it was big enough to be sent to draw beer. Then the mother sat down and exclaimed: "Our Else is clever indeed." Her sobs could be heard above all the others.

Upstairs, Else's father and Hans sat and waited. "I am quite thirsty now, and I must go down to the cellar myself and see what has become of Else and the others." He impatiently started down to the cellar. When he got there, he found them sitting and weeping together, and he too was told that it was because of the child that Else might possibly have and because of the possibility of its being killed by the pickax happening to fall just at the time the child might be sitting underneath it drawing beer. It tore at all their hearts. "How clever is our Else!" he cried as he joined his tears to theirs.

Hans, the intended bridegroom, was upstairs all alone. He sat for a long time. But because nobody had returned from the cellar he decided to go himself and see what was happening. When he got to the cellar, he found all five of them lamenting and crying most pitifully—each louder than the other. "What terrible misfortune has happened?" he inquired.

"Oh, my dear Hans," said Else. "If we marry and have a child and it grows big and we send it down here to draw beer, perhaps that pickax that has been left sticking up there might fall down on the child's head and kill it. How can we help but cry?"

"Well," said Hans, "I cannot think that greater sense than that could be wanted in my household. Because you are so clever, Else, I will have you for my wife." He took her by her hand and led her upstairs, and they had the wedding immediately.

A little while after they were married, Hans said to Else: "I am going to work in order to get money. You go to the field and cut the corn so that we can make some bread."

"Very well. I will do what you ask, dear Hans," agreed Else.

After Hans had gone, Else cooked herself some stew and took it with her into the field. When she got there she thought: Now, what shall I do? Shall I reap first or eat first? All right, I will eat first. Then she ate the stew, and when she could eat no more, she thought, Now, what shall I do? Shall I reap first or sleep first? All right, I will sleep first. She lay down in the corn and fell asleep immediately.

Hans returned home and waited there for a long time, but Else did not come. "My Clever Else is so industrious that she never thinks of coming home and eating and sleeping," he said. But evening drew near and still Else did not come. Hans set out to see how much corn she had cut, but, of course, she had cut no corn at all. There she was lying in the corn asleep with the empty stew pot beside her. Hans ran back to their house and got a bird net with little bells and threw it over her, but she just kept on sleeping. He went home again and locked himself in and sat down on his bench to work.

At last when darkness had fallen, Clever Else woke, got up, and shook herself. Little bells jingled with each movement she made. This frightened her, and she began to doubt whether she were really Clever Else or not, and she started asking herself, Am I, or am I not?" Not knowing what answer to give, she stood for a long while considering. At long last she thought: I will go home to Hans and ask him if I am or not. He is sure to know.

She ran up to the door of her house with the light of the moon to guide her, but it was locked. She knocked on the window and cried, "Hans, is Else within?"

"Yes," answered Hans. "She is in here."

Else was more frightened than ever, and she began to cry. "Oh, dear," she said; "then I am not I." And she left to inquire at another house. But the people heard the jingling of the bells and would not open the door to her. She could get in nowhere, so she ran away beyond the village, and since then no one has seen Clever Else.

The Turnip

(collected by Jacob Grimm and Wilhelm Grimm)

There were once two brothers who served as soldiers. One was rich and the other poor. The poor one, to escape from his poverty, put off his soldier's coat and turned farmer. He dug and hoed his bit of land and sowed it with turnip seed. The seed came up, and one turnip grew there that became large and vigorous and grew visibly bigger and bigger. It seemed as if it would never stop growing. It might have been called the princess of turnips for never was such a turnip seen before—and never will such a turnip be seen again.

It finally became so enormous that it filled a whole cart, and two oxen were required to draw it. The farmer had not the least idea what he was to do with the turnip or whether it would be a fortune to him or a misfortune. At last he thought: If I sell it, what will I get for it? I could eat it myself, but the small turnips would taste just as good. It would be better to take it to the king and make him a present of it.

So he placed it on a cart, harnessed two oxen, took it to the palace, and presented it to the king. "What strange thing is this?" asked the king. "Many wonderful things have come before my eyes, but never such a monster as this! From what seed can this have sprung, or are you a luck child and have met with it by chance?"

"Ah, no!" said the farmer. "No luck child am I. I am a poor soldier, who, because he could no longer support himself, hung his soldier's coat on a nail and took to farming land. I have a brother who is rich and well-known to you, lord king. But I, because I have nothing, am forgotten by everyone."

Then the king felt compassion for him, and said, "You shall be raised from poverty and shall have such gifts from me that you shall be equal to your rich brother." The king bestowed on him much gold, lands, meadows, and herds and made him immensely rich. The wealth of the other brother could not be compared with his.

When the rich brother heard what the poor one had gained for himself with one single turnip, he envied him and thought in every way how he also could get hold of a similar piece of luck. He would, however, set about it in a much wiser way. He took gold and horses and carried them to the king. He wanted to make certain the king would give him a much larger present in return. If his brother had got so much for one turnip, what would he not carry away with him in return for such beautiful things as these? The king accepted his present and said that he had nothing to give him in return that was more rare and excellent than the great turnip.

So the rich man was obliged to put his brother's turnip in a cart and have it taken to his home. When there he did not know on whom to vent his rage and anger. But then bad thoughts came to him, and he resolved to kill his brother. He hired murderers, who were to ambush his brother, and then he went to his brother and said: "Dear brother, I know of a hidden treasure. We will dig it up together and divide it between us." The other agreed to this and accompanied him without suspicion. While they were on their way, however, the murderers fell on him, bound him, and would have hung him from a tree. But just as they were about to do this, loud singing and the sound of a horse's feet were heard in the distance. On this their hearts were filled with terror, and they pushed their prisoner headfirst into the sack, hung it on a branch, and took flight. He, however, worked up there until he had made a hole in the sack through which he could put his head.

The man who was coming by was no other than a traveling student, a young fellow who, on his way through the wood, joyously sang his song. When he who was aloft saw that someone was passing below him, he cried: "Good day! You have come at a lucky time."

The student looked around on every side but did not know where the voice was coming from. At last he called, "Who speaks?"

An answer came from the top of the tree: "Raise your eyes. Here I sit in the Sack of Knowledge. In a short time I have learned great things. Compared with this, all schools are a jest. In a very short time I shall have learned everything and shall descend wiser than all other men. I understand the stars and the signs of the zodiac and the tracks of the winds and the sand of the sea and the healing of illness and the virtues of all herbs, birds, and stones. If you were once within it, you would feel what noble things issue forth from the Sack of Knowledge.

When he heard all this the student was astonished and said: "Blessed be the hour in which I have found you! May not I also enter the sack for a while?"

An unwilling reply came from above: "For a short time I will let you get into it if you reward me and give me good words. You must wait an hour longer, for one thing remains that I must learn before I do it."

The student waited. He became impatient and begged to be allowed to get in at once. His thirst for knowledge was consuming him.

He who was above pretended at last to yield and said, "In order that I may come forth from the house of knowledge you must let it down by the rope, and then you shall enter it."

So the student let the sack down, untied it, and set him free, and then he cried, "Now draw me up at once!" He was about to get into the sack.

"Halt!" cried the other. "That will not do." And he took him by the head and put him upside down into the sack, fastened it, and drew the disciple of wisdom up the tree by the rope. He swung the student in the air and asked: "How goes it with you, my dear fellow? Behold, already you feel wisdom coming and are gaining valuable experience. Keep perfectly quiet until you become wiser." With this he mounted the student's horse and rode away but in an hour's time sent someone to let the student out again.

Prince Hyacinth and the Dear Little Princess
(from *The Blue Fairy Book* edited by Andrew Lang)

Once upon a time there lived a king who was deeply in love with a princess, but she could not marry anyone, because she was under an enchantment. So the king set out to seek a fairy and asked what he could do to win the princess' love. The fairy said to him: "You know that the princess has a great cat that she is very fond of. Whoever is clever enough to tread on that cat's tail is the man she is destined to marry."

The king said to himself that this would not be very difficult, and he left the fairy determined to grind the cat's tail to powder rather than not tread on it at all.

You may imagine that it was not long before he went to see the princess, and puss, as usual, marched in before him, arching his back. The king took a long step and quite thought he had the tail under his foot, but the cat turned round so sharply that he only trod on air. And so it went on for eight days, till the king began to think that this fatal tail must be full of quicksilver—it was never still for a moment.

At last, however, he was lucky enough to come upon puss fast asleep and with his tail conveniently spread out. So the king, without losing a moment, set his foot upon it heavily.

With one terrific yell the cat sprang up and instantly changed into a tall man, who, fixing his angry eyes upon the king, said: "You shall marry the princess because you have been able to break the enchantment, but I will have my revenge. You shall have a son who will never be happy until he finds out that his nose is too long. And if you ever tell anyone what I have just said to you, you shall vanish away instantly, and no one shall ever see you or hear of you again."

Though the king was horribly afraid of the enchanter, he could not help laughing at this threat.

If my son has such a long nose as that, he said to himself, he must always see it or feel it at least, if he is not blind or without hands. But, as the enchanter had vanished, he did not waste any more time in thinking but went to see the princess, who very soon consented to marry him. But after all, they had not been married very long when the king died, and the queen had nothing left to care for but her little son, who was called Hyacinth. The little prince had large blue eyes—the prettiest eyes in the world—and a sweet little mouth. But, alas, his nose was so enormous that it covered half his face. The queen was inconsolable when she saw this great nose, but her ladies assured her that it was not really as large as it looked, that it was a Roman nose, and you had only to open any history to see that every hero had a large nose. The queen, who was devoted to her baby, was pleased with what they told her, and when she looked at Hyacinth again, his nose certainly did not seem to her quite so large.

The prince was brought up with great care. As soon as he could speak, they told him all sorts of dreadful stories about people who had short noses. No one was allowed to go near him whose nose did not more or less resemble his own, and the courtiers, to get into favor with the queen, took to pulling their babies' noses several times every day to make them grow longer. But do what they would, they were nothing by comparison with the prince's.

When he grew sensible, he learned history. And whenever any great prince or beautiful princess was spoken of, his teachers took care to tell him that they had long noses.

His room was hung with pictures of people with very large noses. And the prince grew up so convinced that a long nose was a great beauty, that he would not on any account have had his own a single inch shorter!

When his 20th birthday was past, the queen thought it was time that he should be married, so she commanded that the portraits of several princesses should be brought for him to see, and among the others was a picture of the Dear Little Princess!

Now, she was the daughter of a great king and would some day possess several kingdoms herself. But Prince Hyacinth had not a thought to spare for anything of that sort. He was so much struck with her beauty. The princess, whom he thought quite charming, had, however, a little saucy nose, which, on her face, was the prettiest thing possible, but it was a cause of great embarrassment to the courtiers, who had got into such a habit of laughing at little noses that they sometimes found themselves laughing at hers before they had time to think. But this did not do at all before the prince, who quite failed to see the joke and actually banished two of his courtiers who had dared to mention disrespectfully the Dear Little Princess's tiny nose!

The others, taking warning from this, learned to think twice before they spoke. One even went so far as to tell the prince that, though it was quite true that no man could be worth anything unless he had a long nose, a woman's beauty was a different thing. He added that he knew a learned man who understood Greek and had read in some old manuscripts that the beautiful Cleopatra herself had a "tip-tilted" nose!

The prince made him a splendid present as a reward for this good news and at once sent ambassadors to ask the Dear Little Princess for her hand in marriage. The king, her father, gave his consent, and Prince Hyacinth, who, in his anxiety to see the princess, had gone three leagues to meet her, was just advancing to kiss her hand when, to the horror of all who stood by, the enchanter appeared as suddenly as a flash of lightning and snatched up the Dear Little Princess and whirled her away out of their sight!

The prince was left quite inconsolable and declared that nothing should induce him to go back to his kingdom until he had found her again. He refused to allow any of his courtiers to follow him and then mounted his horse and rode sadly away, letting the animal choose his own path.

So it happened that he came presently to a great plain, across which he rode all day long without seeing a single house. Horse and rider had grown terribly hungry, when, as the night fell, the prince caught sight of a light that seemed to shine from a cavern.

He rode up to it and saw a little old woman who appeared to be at least 100 years old.

She put on her spectacles to look at Prince Hyacinth, but it was quite a long time before she could fix them securely because her nose was so very short.

The prince and the fairy (for that was who she was) had no sooner looked at each other than they went into fits of laughter and cried at the same moment, "Oh, what a funny nose!"

"Not so funny as your own," said Prince Hyacinth to the fairy. "But, madam, I beg you to leave the consideration of our noses—such as they are—and to be good enough to give me something to eat, for I am starving and so is my poor horse."

"With all my heart," said the fairy. "Though your nose is so ridiculous, you are, nevertheless, the son of my best friend. I loved your father as if he had been my brother. Now he had a very handsome nose!"

"And pray what does mine lack?" asked the prince.

"Oh! It doesn't lack anything," replied the fairy. "On the contrary quite, there is only too much of it. But never mind, one may be a very worthy man though his nose is too long. I was telling you that I was your father's friend. He often came to see me in the old times, and you must know that I was very pretty in those days—at least he used to say so. I should like to tell you of a conversation we had the last time I ever saw him."

"Indeed," said the prince, "when I have supped, it will give me the greatest pleasure to hear it. But consider, madam, I beg of you, that I have had nothing to eat today."

"The poor boy is right," said the fairy. "I was forgetting. Come in, then, and I will give you some supper, and while you are eating, I can tell you my story in a very few words—for I do not like endless tales myself. Too long a tongue is worse than too long a nose, and I remember when I was young that I was so much admired for not being a great chatterer. They used to tell the queen, my mother, that it was so. For though you see what I am now, I was the daughter of a great king. My father—"

"Your father, I dare say, got something to eat when he was hungry!" interrupted the prince.

"Oh, certainly," answered the fairy, "and you also shall have supper directly. I only just wanted to tell you—"

"But I really cannot listen to anything until I have had something to eat," cried the prince, who was getting quite angry. But then, remembering that he had better be polite as he much needed the fairy's help, he added: "I know that in the pleasure of listening to you I should quite forget my own hunger. But my horse—who cannot hear you—must really be fed!"

The fairy was very much flattered by this compliment and said, calling to her servants: "You shall not wait another minute. You are so polite, and in spite of the enormous size of your nose, you are really very agreeable."

Plague take the old lady! How she does go on about my nose! said the prince to himself. One would almost think that mine had taken all the extra length that hers lacks! If I were not so hungry, I would soon have done with this chatterbox who thinks she talks very little! How stupid people are not to see their own faults! That comes of being a princess: She has been spoiled by flatterers, who have made her believe that she is quite a moderate talker!

Meanwhile the servants were putting the supper on the table, and the prince was much amused to hear the fairy, who asked them many questions simply for the pleasure of hearing herself speak. Especially he noticed one maid who, no matter what was being said, always contrived to praise her mistress' wisdom.

Well! he thought, as he ate his supper, I'm very glad I came here. This just shows me how sensible I have been in never listening to flatterers. People of that sort praise us to our faces without shame and hide our faults or change them into virtues. For my part, I never will be taken in by them. I know my own defects, I hope.

Poor Prince Hyacinth! He really believed what he said and had no idea that the people who had praised his nose were laughing at him, just as the fairy's maid was laughing at her. For the prince had seen the maid laugh shyly when she could do so without the fairy's noticing her.

However, he said nothing, and presently, when his hunger began to be appeased, the fairy said: "My dear prince, might I beg you to move a little more that way, for your nose casts such a shadow that I really cannot see what I have on my plate. Ah! Thanks. Now let us speak of your father. When I went to his court, he was only a little boy. But was 40 years ago, and I have been in this desolate place ever since. Tell me, what goes on nowadays." Are the ladies as fond of amusement as ever? In my time one saw them at parties, theaters, balls, and promenades every day. Dear me! What a long nose you have! I cannot get used to it!"

"Really, madam," said the prince, "I wish you would leave off mentioning my nose. It cannot matter to you what it is like. I am quite satisfied with it and have no wish to have it shorter. One must take what is given one."

"Now you are angry with me, my poor Hyacinth," said the fairy, "and I assure you that I did not mean to vex you. On the contrary, I wished to do you a service. However, though I really cannot help your nose being a shock to me, I will try not to say anything about it. I will even try to think that you have an ordinary nose. To tell the truth, it would make three reasonable ones."

The prince, who was no longer hungry, grew so impatient at the fairy's continual remarks about his nose that at last he threw himself upon his horse and rode hastily away. But wherever he went in his journeys he thought the people were mad, for they all talked of his nose. Yet he could not bring himself to admit that it was too long, for he had been so used all his life to hearing it called handsome.

The old fairy, who wished to make him happy, at last hit upon a plan. She shut the Dear Little Princess up in a palace of crystal and put this palace down where the prince could not fail to find it. His joy at seeing the princess again was extreme, and he set to work with all his might to try to break her prison. But in spite of all his efforts he failed utterly. In despair he thought at least that he would try to get near enough to speak to the Dear Little Princess, who, on her part, stretched out her hand that he might kiss it. But turn which way he might, he never could raise it to his lips, for his long nose always prevented it. For the first time he realized how long it really was and exclaimed, "Well, it must be admitted that my nose is too long!"

In an instant the crystal prison flew into a thousand splinters, and the old fairy, taking the Dear Little Princess by the hand, said to the prince: "Now, say if you are not very much obliged to me. Much good it was for me to talk to you about your nose! You would never have found out how extraordinary it was if it had not hindered you from doing what you wanted to. You see how self-love keeps us from knowing our own defects of mind and body. Our reason tries in vain to show them to us, but we refuse to see them till we find them in the way of our interests."

Prince Hyacinth, whose nose was now just like anyone else's, did not fail to profit by the lesson he had received. He married the Dear Little Princess, and they lived happily ever after.

(Reprinted by permission of the publisher.)

Little Thumb

(from *The Blue Fairy Book* edited by Andrew Lang)

There was, once upon a time, a man and his wife, fagot makers by trade, who had seven children—all boys. The eldest was but 10 years old and the youngest only 7.

They were very poor, and their seven children incommoded them greatly, because not one of them was able to earn his bread. That which gave them yet more uneasiness was that the youngest was of a very puny constitution, and scarcely ever spoke a word, which made them take for stupidity what was a sign of good sense. He was very little and when born no bigger than one's thumb, which made him be called Little Thumb.

The poor child bore the blame of whatsoever was done amiss in the house and, guilty or not, was always in the wrong. He was, notwithstanding, more cunning and had a far greater share of wisdom than all his brothers put together. And if he spoke little, he heard and thought the more.

There happened now to come a very bad year, and the famine was so great that these poor people resolved to rid themselves of their children. One evening when they were all in bed and the fagot maker was sitting with his wife at the fire, he said to her with his heart ready to burst with grief: "Thou seest plainly that we are not able to keep our children, and I cannot see them starve to death before my face. I am resolved to lose them in the wood tomorrow, which may very easily be done. While they are busy in tying up the fagots, we may run away and leave them without their taking any notice."

"Ah!" cried out his wife. "And canst thou thyself have the heart to take thy children out along with thee on purpose to lose them?"

In vain did her husband represent to her their extreme poverty. But she would not consent to the deed. She was indeed poor, but she was their mother. However, having considered what a grief it would be to her to see them perish with hunger, she at last consented and went to bed all in tears.

Little Thumb heard every word that had been spoken, for observing, as he lay in his bed, that they were talking very busily, he had got up softly and hid himself under his father's stool so that he might hear what they said without being seen. He went to bed again but did not sleep a wink all the rest of the night thinking on what he had to do. He got up early in the morning and went to the river, where he filled his pockets full of small white pebbles, and then he returned home.

They all went abroad, but Little Thumb never told his brothers one syllable of what he knew. They went into a very thick forest, where they could not see one another at ten paces distance. The fagot maker began to cut wood, and the children gathered the sticks to make fagots. Their father and mother, seeing them busy at their work, got away from them insensibly and ran away from them all at once along a byway through the winding bushes.

When the children saw they were left alone, they began to cry as loud as they could. Little Thumb let them cry on, knowing very well how to get home again, for as he came he had taken care to drop all along the way the little white pebbles he had in his pockets. Then he said to them: "Be not afraid, brothers. Father and mother have left us here, but I will lead you home again. Follow me."

They did so, and he took them home by the very same way they had come into the forest. They dared not go in, but sat themselves down at the door, listening to what their father and mother were talking about.

The very moment the fagot maker and his wife were got home the lord of the manor sent them ten crowns, which he had owed them a long while and which they had never expected. This gave them new life, for the poor people were almost famished. The fagot maker sent his wife immediately to the butcher's. As it was a long while since they had eaten a bit, she bought thrice as much meat as would sup two people. When they had eaten, the woman said: "Alas! Where are now our poor children? They would make a good feast of what we have left here. But it was you, William, who had a mind to lose them. I told you we should repent of it. What are they now doing in the forest? Alas, dear God! The wolves have perhaps already eaten them up. Thou art very inhuman thus to have lost thy children."

The fagot maker grew at last quite out of patience, for she repeated it above 20 times that they should repent of it and that she was in the right of it for so saying. He threatened to beat her if she did not hold her tongue. It was not that the fagot maker was not, perhaps, more vexed than his wife but that she teased him and that he was of the humor of a great many others who love wives who speak well but think those very importunate who are continually doing so. She was half drowned in tears, crying out: "Alas! Where are now my children, my poor children?"

She spoke this so very loud that the children, who were at the gate, began to cry out all together: "Here we are! Here we are!"

She ran immediately to open the door and said, hugging them: "I am glad to see you, my dear children. You are very hungry and weary. And my poor Peter, thou art horribly bemired. Come in and let me clean thee."

Now, you must know that Peter was her eldest son, whom she loved above all the rest, because he was somewhat carroty, as she herself was. They sat down to supper and ate with such a good appetite as pleased both Father and Mother, whom they acquainted how frightened they were in the forest, speaking almost always all together. The good folks were extremely glad to see their children once more at home, and this joy continued while the 10 crowns lasted. But when the money was all gone, they fell again into their former uneasiness and resolved to lose them again. And that they might be the surer of doing it, they carried them to a much greater distance than before.

They talked of this so secretly, but they were overheard by Little Thumb, who made account to get out of this difficulty as well as the former. But though he got up very betimes in the morning to go and pick up some little pebbles, he was disappointed, for he found the house door double locked and was at a stand about what to do. When their father had given each of them a piece of bread for their breakfast, he fancied he might make use of this instead of the pebbles and throw it in little bits all along the way they should pass. And so he put the bread in his pocket.

Their father and mother took them into the thickest and most obscure part of the forest, when, stealing away into a bypath, they there left them. Little Thumb was not very uneasy at it, for he thought he could easily find the way again by means of his bread, which he had scattered all along as he came. But he was very much surprised when he could not find so much as one crumb: The birds had come and had eaten it up—every bit. They were now in great affliction, for the farther they went the more they were out of their way, and they became more and more bewildered in the forest.

Night now came on, and there arose a terrible high wind, which made them dreadfully afraid. They fancied they heard on every side of them the howling of wolves coming to eat them up. They scarce dared to speak or turn their heads. After this, it rained very hard, which wetted them to the skin. Their feet slipped at every step they took, and they fell into the mire, whence they got up in a very dirty pickle. Their hands were quite benumbed.

Little Thumb climbed up to the top of a tree to see if he could discover anything. Having turned his head about on every side, he saw at last a glimmering light, like that of a candle, but a long way from the forest. He came down, and, when upon the ground, he could see it no more, which grieved him sadly. However, having walked for some time with his brothers toward that side on which he had seen the light, he perceived it again as he came out of the wood.

They came at last to the house where this candle was, but not without an abundance of fear: For very often they lost sight of it, which happened every time they came into a bottom. They knocked at the door, and a good woman came and opened it. She asked them what they would have.

Little Thumb told her they were poor children who had been lost in the forest and who desired to lodge there for God's sake.

The woman, seeing them so very pretty, began to weep and said to them: "Alas! Poor babies, whither are ye come? Do ye know that this house belongs to a cruel ogre who eats up little children?"

"Ah, dear madam," answered Little Thumb (who trembled every joint of him, as well as his brothers), "what shall we do? To be sure the wolves of the forest will devour us tonight if you refuse us to lie here. And so we would rather the gentleman should eat us. Perhaps he may take pity upon us—especially if you please to beg it of him."

The ogre's wife, who believed she could conceal them from her husband till morning, let them come in and took them to warm themselves at a very good fire, for there was a whole sheep upon the spit that was roasting for the ogre's supper.

As they began to be a little warm they heard three or four great raps at the door. The ogre was home. Upon this she hid them under the bed and went to open the door. The ogre presently asked if supper was ready and the wine drawn, and then he sat himself down to table. The sheep was as yet all raw and bloody, but he liked it the better for that. He sniffed about to the right and left, saying, "I smell fresh meat."

"What you smell so," said his wife, "must be the calf that I have just now killed and flayed."

"I smell fresh meat, I tell thee once more," replied the ogre, looking crossly at his wife. "And there is something here that I do not understand."

As he spoke these words he got up from the table and went directly to the bed.

"Aha!" said he. "I see then how thou wouldst cheat me, thou cursed woman. I know not why I do not eat thee up too, but it is well for thee that thou art a tough old carrion. Here is good game, which comes very luckily to entertain three ogres of my acquaintance who are to pay me a visit in a day or two."

With that he dragged them out from under the bed, one by one. The poor children fell upon their knees and begged his pardon. But they had to do with one of the most cruel ogres in the world, who, far from having any pity on them, had already devoured them with his eyes and who had told his wife they would be delicate eating when tossed up with good savory sauce. He then took a great knife and, coming up to these poor children, whetted it upon a great whetstone that he held in his left hand. He had already taken hold of one of them when his wife said to him: "What need you do it now? Is it not time enough tomorrow?"

"Hold your prating," said the ogre. "They will eat the tenderer."

"But you have so much meat already," replied his wife. "You have no occasion. Here are a calf, two sheep, and half a hog."

"That is true," said the ogre. "Give them their bellyful that they may not fall away, and put them to bed."

The good woman was overjoyed at this and gave them a good supper. But they were so much afraid they could not eat a bit. As for the ogre, he sat down again to drink, being highly pleased that he had got wherewithal to treat his friends. He drank a dozen glasses more than ordinary, which got up into his head and obliged him to go to bed.

The ogre had seven daughters, all little children, and these young ogresses had all of them very fine complexions, because they used to eat fresh meat like their father. But they had little gray eyes—quite round—hooked noses, and very long, sharp teeth, standing at a good distance from each other. They were not as yet over and above mischievousness, but they promised very fair for it, for they had already bitten little children so that they might suck their blood.

They had been put to bed early, with every one a crown of gold upon her head. There was in the same chamber a bed of the like bigness, and it was into this bed the ogre's wife put the seven little boys, after which she went to bed to her husband.

Little Thumb, who had observed that the ogre's daughters had crowns of gold upon their heads and was afraid lest the ogre should repent his not killing them, got up about midnight and, taking his brothers' bonnets and his own, went very softly and put them upon the heads of the seven little ogresses after having taken off their crowns of gold, which he put upon his own head and his brothers' so that the ogre might take them for his daughters and his daughters for the little boys whom he wanted to kill.

All this succeeded according to his desire. For the ogre, waking about midnight and sorry that he deferred to do that till morning which he might have done overnight, threw himself hastily out of bed and took his great knife.

"Let us see," said he, "how our little rogues do, and not make two jobs of the matter."

He then went up, groping all the way, into his daughters' chamber and coming to the bed where the little boys lay—and who were every soul of them fast asleep, except Little Thumb, who was terribly afraid when he found the ogre fumbling about his head, as he had done about his brothers'—the ogre, feeling the golden crowns said: "I should have made a fine piece of work of it, truly. I find I drank too much last night."

Then he went to the bed where the girls lay and found the boys' little bonnets.

"Ah!" said he. "My merry lads, are you there? Let us work as we ought."

And saying these words without more ado, he cut the throats of all his seven daughters.

Well pleased with what he had done, he went to bed again to his wife. So soon as Little Thumb heard the ogre snore, he waked his brothers, and bade them put on their clothes presently and follow him. They stole down softly into the garden and got over the wall. They kept running about all night and trembled all the while without knowing which way they went.

The ogre, when he awoke, said to his wife, "Go upstairs and dress those young rascals who came here last night."

The ogress was very much surprised at this goodness of her husband, not dreaming after what manner she should dress them. But thinking that he had ordered her to go and put on their clothes, she went up and was strangely astonished when she perceived her seven daughters killed and weltering in their blood.

She fainted away, for this is the first expedient almost all women find in such cases. The ogre, fearing his wife would be too long in doing what he had ordered, went up himself to help her. He was no less amazed than his wife at this frightful spectacle.

"Ah! What have I done?" cried he. "The wretches shall pay for it, and that instantly."

He threw a pitcher of water upon his wife's face, and having brought her to herself he cried, "Give me quickly my boots of seven leagues so that I may go and catch them."

He went out, and, having run over a vast deal of ground, both on this side and that, he came at last into the very road where the poor children were—and not above 100 paces from their father's house. They espied the ogre, who went at one step from mountain to mountain and over rivers as easily as the narrowest kennels. Little Thumb, seeing a hollow rock near the place where they were, made his brothers hide themselves in it and crowded into it himself, minding always what would become of the ogre.

The ogre, who found himself much tired with his long and fruitless journey (for these boots of seven leagues greatly fatigued the wearer), had a great mind to rest himself and, by chance, went to sit down upon the rock where the little boys had hidden themselves. As it was impossible that he could be more weary than he was, he fell asleep, and after reposing himself some time he began to snore so frightfully that the poor children were no less afraid of him than when he had held up his great knife and was going to cut their throats. Little Thumb was not so much frightened as his brothers and told them that they should run away immediately toward home while the ogre was asleep so soundly and that they should not be in any pain about him. They took his advice and got home presently. Little Thumb went up to the ogre, pulled off his boots gently, and put them on his own legs. The boots were very long and large, but as they were fairies, they had the gift of becoming big and little, according to the legs of those who wore them, so they fit his feet and legs as well as if they had been made on purpose for him. He went immediately to the ogre's house, where he saw the ogre's wife crying bitterly for the loss of her murdered daughters.

"Your husband," said Little Thumb, "is in very great danger of being taken by a gang of thieves who have sworn to kill him if he does not give them all his gold and silver. The very moment they held their daggers at his throat he perceived me and desired me to come and tell you the condition he is in so that you should give me whatsoever he has of value without retaining any one thing. Otherwise, they will kill him without mercy. And as his case is very pressing, he desired me to make use (you see I have them on) of his boots so that I might make the more haste and to show you that I do not impose upon you."

The good woman, being sadly frightened, gave him all she had, for this ogre was a very good husband though he used to eat up little children. Little Thumb, having thus got all the ogre's money, went home to his father's house, where he was received with an abundance of joy.

There are many people who do not agree in this circumstance and pretend that Little Thumb never robbed the ogre at all and that he only thought he might very justly, and with a safe conscience, take off his boots of seven leagues because he made no other use of them than to run after little children. These folks affirm that they are very well assured of this, and the more as having drunk and eaten often at the fagot maker's house. They aver that when Little Thumb had taken off the ogre's boots, he went to court, where he was informed that they were very much in pain about a certain army, which was 200 leagues off, and the success of a battle. He went, say they, to the king, and told him that if he desired it, he would bring him news from the army before night.

The king promised him a great sum of money upon that condition. Little Thumb was as good as his word and returned that very same night with the news. And that first expedition causing him to be known, he got whatever he pleased, for the king paid him very well for carrying his orders to the army. After some time carrying on the business of a messenger and gaining thereby great wealth, he went home to his father, where it was impossible to express the joy they were all in at his return. He made the whole family very easy, bought places for his father and brothers, and, by that means, settled them very handsomely in the world and, in the meantime, made his court to perfection.

(Reprinted by permission of the publisher.)

Discussion

The school-related fears of children are a startlingly large portion of the stressful events in their lives. Of the 20 listed fears, eight of them can be connected to school. They are fear of being retained academically, fear of having a poor report card, fear of being sent to the principal, fear of being ridiculed in class, fear of moving to a new school, fear of not making 100 on a test, fear of being picked last on teams, and fear of giving a class report.

Children, like the Ugly Duckling, are constantly striving to conform and be like everyone else. They try to gain approval and acceptance. Children want to fit in with other children as well as satisfy academic expectations of teachers, principals, and parents. Family perceptions of and reactions to children's schoolwork is a big factor in school-related fears. One startling report from Cobb County, Georgia, stated that child abuse doubled in the three days after school grades are issued. This school business is serious stuff.

Youngsters need to feel accepted and competent, or else frustrations and problems set in. A book, along with the Ugly Duckling story, that would make a great discussion starter for kids concerning being different is *Just Like Everyone Else* by Karla Kuskin. When I initially read this little book, I was cynical about its message. It seemed that the author was perpetuating every stereotype as to what a family is, does, wears, and eats. I got more agitated as I read it—until the surprise ending jolted me into laughter. *Just Like Everyone Else* is one of the great predictable stories with an unexpected ending. It is a wonderful book to share.

Since there are so many aspects of life in school that are stressful, it is vital to listen to children as they talk about school. There is no such thing as something that is not important. As adults, we may feel some of their concerns are trivial, but to children they are important. Children must learn to cope with these everyday events, and we can help them if we take the time to pay attention to their worries and to encourage them to brainstorm ways they might handle these problems. Embarrassment or humiliation can be an especially stinging blow to a child's emerging sense of worth and when felt can act as two of the most common triggers of suicide. These injuries to self-esteem can come to define children's whole identity.

Activities

- Adults often have school-fear dreams. One 75-year-old ex-teacher still dreams it is December, and she has not yet taught all her first-graders to read! Have the children interview adults for similar dreams that they might compile in a class book of adult school-fear dreams.

- Most of these school fears appear in comic strips. *Calvin and Hobbes* by Bill Watterson is a rich source for these topics. In this comic strip see how many fears related to school you can find used as subject matter.

- Collect Charles M. Schultz's *Peanuts* comic strips for two weeks from the daily newspaper. Analyze them for what school fears they depict. A good time to do this is in the fall when schools are opening.

- Why has *Peanuts* been so popular for so long? Are the strips funny? Sad? Do they help solve problems?

- Interview people to find out why they like *Calvin and Hobbes* and *Peanuts*. What do they like about them?

- Look through the comic-strip section of the daily newspaper and collect and file cartoons that deal with school fears. How many different school fears can be identified?

- As you read books and stories, list any that are connected with school fears. Keep a file of these, and later share them. Did reading these stories help in any way with any fears? If so, how?

- Because many of these school fears are found in just a few pieces of literature, can you write a story, poem, or song about one that troubles you? Share these with others.

- How could you help another student who is having problems in school?

- Write a readers' theater script for one of the following books, and share it with other groups.

Bibliography

Baehr, Patricia. *School Isn't Fair.* Illustrations by R. W. Alley. New York: Alladin Books, 1992.
    A four-year-old boy describes all the unfair things that happen to him during a school day.

Butterworth, Nick, and Mick Inkpen. *The School Trip.* New York: Delacorte, 1990.
    Matthew Tibbs has problems on this eagerly awaited school trip to the Natural History Museum. The story is full of gentle chaos and will maybe help others who have ever had discomfort on school trips.

Carrick, Carol. *Some Friend.* Illustrations by Donald Carrick. New York: Clarion, 1980.
    Mike has a problem with his best friend, Rob. Rob always has to be the top dog. This is an active story sensitively attuned to inner tensions.

____. *What a Wimp!* Illustrations by Donald Carrick. New York: Clarion, 1983.
    Barney's parents have divorced, and his mother moves her boys to a place she knew as a youngster. Barney's life is made miserable by Lenny the bully, and Barney knows he will have to find his own way to deal with Lenny.

Cleary, Beverly. *Dear Mr. Henshaw.* Illustrations by Paul O. Zelinsky. New York: Morrow, 1983.
    Ten-year-old Leigh, a new sixth-grader in a new school, has to do an author report for class. In his letters to his favorite author he reveals his problems in coping with his parents' divorce, being the new boy in school, and generally finding his own place in the world. This Newbery Award-winning book is one of the few Newbery winners that speaks directly to children and has become a favorite with them.

Cole, Joanna. *Don't Call Me Names.* Illustrations by Lynn Munsinger. New York: Random House, 1990.
    Nell is afraid of Mike and Joe because they always tease her and make fun of her until the day she stands up to them on behalf of her friend Nicky.

Cooper, Ilene. *Frances in the Fourth Grade*. New York: Knopf, 1991.

Frances has the courage to take on the fourth grade as long as her best friend, Bonnie, is by her side. What happens when Bonnie moves away?

Estes, Eleanor. *The Hundred Dresses*. Illustrations by Louis Slobodkin. New York: Harcourt, 1944.

Eleanor Estes was one of the first authors to write about children's relationships in their closed world. A poor girl, new to the school, boasts that she really has 100 lovely dresses at home. A good book for initiating a discussion about fitting in with others in school.

Fitzhugh, Louise. *Harriet the Spy*. New York: Harper, 1964.

This book wears well over the years. The concerns are so universal and timeless. Harriet is a note taker and a spy. Her writings are found, and the kids in school turn on her for her unkind observations about them. Harriet learns a huge lesson.

Giff, Patricia Reilly. Kids of Polk Street Series. New York: Dell.

There are 12 titles in this series, and they all take a playful look at a classroom full of kids and their school adventures.

Hale, Irina. *How I Found a Friend*. New York: Viking, 1992.

Teddy bears and hats provide the opening for a friendship between two young children.

Hanft, Philip. *Never Fear, Flip the Dip Is Here*. Illustrations by Thomas B. Allen. New York: Dial, 1991.

Flip wants to play baseball, but the neighborhood kids do not want to play baseball with Flip. He cannot catch. He cannot throw. Flip meets a former minor-league ball player who coaches Flip. Through his coach's encouragement, Flip learns not only about playing ball but about the value of friendship and self-confidence as well.

Heide, Florence Parry. *The Shrinking of Treehorn*. Illustrations by Edward Gorey. New York: Holiday House, 1971.

Treehorn is shrinking, but people refuse to pay attention. His teacher sends him to the principal for his shrinking behavior. The visit with the principal is classic.

___. *Treehorn's Treasure*. Illustrations by Edward Gorey. New York: Holiday House, 1981.

Treehorn discovers a tree that grows money. When he tries to share his discovery with others, Treehorn is ignored repeatedly but remains undaunted in this amusing story.

Kraus, Robert. *Spider's First Day at School.* New York: Scholastic, 1987.

Spider is nervous about attending Bugsville School for the first time. The bedbugs are mean to him, and Fly is suspicious of him. At recess a friendly Ladybug asks Spider to join in a football game, and when he helps to win the game, he also wins over Fly and the bedbugs.

Kuskin, Karla. *Just Like Everyone Else.* New York: Harper & Row, 1959.

Jonathan James is just like everyone else. He does the same things as everyone else. In fact, everything about him is just like everyone else—that is, until he leaves for school.

Lord, Bette Bao. *In the Year of the Boar and Jackie Robinson.* Illustrations by Marc Simont. New York: Harper & Row, 1984.

A young Asian girl new to the United States and to school learns all about America and what is important. Her interpretation of what everyone is saying in the Pledge of Allegiance is a classic example of how kids use familiar experiences to make sense of the unknown.

Park, Barbara. *Maxie, Rosie, and Earl—Partners in Grime.* Illustrations by Alexander Strogart. New York: Knopf, 1991.

Three likable misfits end up in the principal's office for different reasons. Life in the fourth grade seems totally unfair. This trio finds friendship in the oddest of places.

Paulsen, Gary. *The Boy Who Owned the School.* New York: Orchard Books, 1990.

Jacob Freisten, often in a fog, tries to ease through high school unnoticed, but a beautiful classmate takes notice of him, and his life begins to change.

Robinson, Barbara. *The Best Christmas Pageant Ever.* Illustrations by Judith Gwyn Brown. New York: Harper & Row, 1972.

This is a wonderful story of the ubiquitous school programs. I dare you to read it and not remember pageants past.

Shreve, Susan. *The Flunking of Joshua T. Bates.* Illustrations by Diane DeGroat. New York: Knopf, 1993.

Joshua faces one of childhood's greatest nightmares—flunking third grade—but he comes through with the help of a sympathetic teacher.

Smith-Moore, J. J. *Sally Small.* Los Angeles: Price Stern Sloan, 1988.

Sally learns that good things come in small packages—including herself—after her wish to be tall is granted.

Spinelli, Jerry. *Fourth Grade Rats.* New York: Scholastic, 1991.
  Suds learns that his best friend is wrong. You do not have to be a tough guy, a "rat," to be a grown-up fourth-grader.

Stolz, Mary. *Bully of Barkham Street.* Illustrations by Leonard Shortall. New York: Harper, 1963.

_____. *Dog on Barkham Street.* Illustrations by Leonard Shortall. New York: Harper, 1960.
  This book and *Bully of Barkham Street* cover the same incidents, but each is told from the point of view of the bully and the youngster being bullied.

Wild, Margaret. *The Very Best of Friends.* Illustrations by Julie Vivas. San Diego, Calif.: Harcourt Brace Jovanovich, 1990.
  After the death of his beloved owner, a cat named William wins the heart of his grieving mistress and shows her what a good friend a cat can be.

Zolotow, Charlotte. *William's Doll.* Illustrations by William Pene Du Bois. New York: Harper & Row, 1972.
  Though William is taunted by the boy next door and his own brother for wanting a doll, William's grandmother finds a real reason for him to have one.

Being Caught in a Theft

The Old Thief
(from Korea)

There once was an old thief in Korea who thought he was too clever to ever get caught. As usually happens, when someone gets too confident, they get careless, and so it was with this thief. He was stealing some spices from a shop, and this time he was caught by the shop owner. Since everyone knew the old thief, there was great pleasure when the police led him into court to be faced by the most severe of all the judges. The judge pronounced an extremely heavy fine, which, of course, the old thief could not pay, so the judge sentenced him to a five-year jail sentence.

The thief planned to escape from jail, but he could not find any possible way to get out of the jail. I'll just have to come up with another way to get out of here, he thought. Early the next morning he called for the jail keeper to come.

"I need to see the king," he demanded. "Take me to him immediately!"

The jail keeper roared with laughter at this request and laughed so that his sides hurt. "What makes you think the king would want to see you?" he sneered when his laughing calmed down.

The old thief ignored all the laughter and contempt and replied: "Tell him I have a gift for him. This gift is one of extraordinary value. Tell the king what I have said."

The thief seemed so serious that he convinced the jail keeper that it was important for him to contact the king. So the jail keeper arranged to set up an audience with the king for the very next afternoon.

The thief was taken to the royal palace, and there he came face-to-face with the stern, imposing king who was seated on an enormous throne. "Well, I hear you have a special gift for me," the king snapped. "What is it? Hurry now, I don't have time to waste with the likes of you."

The wily thief saw that he was not just in the presence of the king, but also the prime minister, the general—who was the head of the military—and the secretary of state were there along with the jail keeper.

"Sire, Your Majestic Majesty," said the thief with a humble voice, "I am here to present you with a rare and valuable gift." With that the thief reached into his pocket and withdrew a tiny box, wrapped in gold paper with silver ribbons. He took this elegant package out with a flourish and handed it to the king.

The king took the package and snatched the wrappings off the box, opened it, and looked inside. His face flushed red and he bellowed in rage: "What is the meaning of this? How dare you bring me an ordinary plum pit?"

"Yes," agreed the thief. "It is a plum pit but not an ordinary one. He who plants this unique pit will reap nothing but golden plums."

Everyone in the room gasped at the same time with this news. Finally the king mused: "If that is the case, why did you steal? Why did you not plant this pit yourself and have the gold yourself?"

"Ah, there is a very good reason, Your Highness," answered the thief. "You see, only people who have never stolen or cheated can reap the golden plums. Otherwise, the tree will only bear ordinary plums. That is why I could never plant it and lose its magic." As he said this, the thief smiled and put on his most deferent manner. "That is why I have brought this pit to you because certainly you, oh mighty king, have never stolen anything or cheated."

The king sat on his throne and he seemed to slump a bit. Quietly the king said, "Alas, I am afraid that I am not the right person for this special plum pit." His regret was obvious. No matter what faults the king had, at least he was a relatively honest man.

Everyone gathered in the throne room gasped. The silent king remembered how he had stolen some shiny coins from his father's treasure chest when he was a little boy.

The thief brightened and suggested, "Perhaps the prime minister should plant the plum—."

Before the thief got the whole sentence out of his mouth, the prime minister blushed bright red and stuttered, "Impossible!" Only he knew that he had often accepted bribes from people who wanted to ingratiate themselves with the king or who wanted high-paying positions in the government. Obviously, the pit would not work for him either.

The thief turned to the general who was covered with medals and ribbons and said, "You then, general."

The general lowered his eyes and muttered, "No, no, not me." How could he explain that he had cheated his soldiers of part of their pay and become an enormously rich man doing this?

The thief took a step toward the secretary of state and looked him in the eyes. "Oh dear, oh dear, not me either." Actually the secretary of state was an honorable old man troubled with his conscience. Like the others he too had accepted money in exchange for governmental favors.

"Then it is decided," stated the thief. "Jail keeper, you must be the one to plant the plum pit."

The solemn jail keeper silently shook his head and shrugged his shoulders. With hesitation the jail keeper said, "No, I am not the right man either." As he admitted this he remembered how he had treated prisoners according to whether they gave him money or not. Those that gave him money seemed to get better food and cells than others.

The thief refused to accept defeat and gazed at the other court officials, who each awkwardly rejected the wonderful plum pit that would give them golden fruit forever.

The room became entirely quiet. No one said anything, but each of the court officials was embarrassed and uncomfortable. The stillness was broken by the laughter of the thief. "So, even you fine gentlemen steal, cheat, and embezzle, and yet none of you is in jail!" exclaimed the thief. "Because I have stolen some spices and could not pay my fine, I am to lose five whole years of my life." As he said this he looked at each of the people in the room earnestly. For quite some time the room remained quiet, and the people in it were silent with shame.

With a low voice, the king spoke: "I think it might be a good thing if we all contribute to this man's fine so that he can become a free man again. Jail is a harsh punishment for what he has done." One by one, each of the men went up to the king and placed some money at his feet.

"Come here, my man," gently ordered the king to the thief. "Here is money enough to pay your fine. You are free. You have also reminded us all of some important things that we will always remember. Thank you for teaching us this lesson."

The clever old thief, with nothing more than a plum pit and his quick wit to help him, was once more a free man.

Discussion

This folktale clearly makes the point that there is probably no one on Earth who has not stolen or cheated at one point in their lives. That does not make it right, of course. It just makes obvious a fact of life. We are not talking about major theft and premeditated theft but the kind of stealing that children cannot resist. Have you ever taken change from your parents? Could you resist the pencil, toy, or appealing object that belonged to someone else? I think if we honestly look back, we will remember taking something that belonged to another person.

The worst thing of all is getting caught in the act. This moment of being caught makes us become honest quite quickly. There is nothing more frightening for the average little kid than to get caught red-handed. In all honesty, my particular failing was erasers. I remember the moment vividly still when a store clerk took me, a five-year-old, to the office (eraser in hand) and called my parents and, I was sure at the time, ruined my life forever. Erasers never looked so appealing to me again. My parents had me take money from my piggy bank to repay them for what they had paid the store. It was a lesson that stuck with me for life.

As a teacher, one of the most difficult times in school was when one child would accuse another of stealing something from them. It was important to avoid calling someone a thief or liar during these times but to try instead to turn it into a learning situation for both the accuser and the accused.

Older youngsters steal for different reasons. In a 1992 survey done by students of Cherry Creek High School, Colorado, the students found that 8 out of 10 people surveyed said that they had been with someone who had shoplifted. Three out of 4 said that they had shoplifted, and fewer than 2 out of 10 had ever been caught. Students reported they shoplifted because of peer pressure or just for the excitement of getting away with a crime. Those who shoplifted for excitement felt little guilt. This survey is all the more surprising because the students come from an above-average economic level. They did not shoplift because of any felt financial need.

On December 7, 1992, the most embarrassing shoplifting incident was international in scope. Houston's Texas Southern University marching band, on a goodwill trip to Japan, had turned their Tokyo tour into a shoplifting spree, making off with $22,000 in loot from stores. One bystander even claimed that a student had brazenly videotaped enraged merchants chasing the thieves to their buses.

When Japanese police told the Americans that the buses would not leave for the airport until the items were returned, more than 80 CD players, pocket recorders, miniature televisions, and electric razors suddenly—and anonymously—were handed over to the police. The incident profoundly embarrassed the university and has given rise to concerns that the students' behavior will further tarnish the negative opinion of Americans already held by many Japanese.

Clearly, our young people need to develop inner responsibility toward theft. It is extremely important to praise youngsters when they demonstrate moral courage. If a youngster does not go along with others who are doing something wrong, be lavish in your praise!

Activities

- Have the youngsters research how other cultures discipline thieves. How have thieves been handled in other times? For instance, how were horse thieves treated in the old days of the West? Students can share what they discover by developing cartoons about it.

- Have youngsters read *The Great Gilly Hopkins* and discuss her behavior and attitude. What caused her to steal?

- What can communities do to discourage shoplifting?

- In 1992, the Los Angeles riots involved mass store break-ins and stealing. How can such behavior be avoided in the future? Is such action ever justified? (For example, think of riots after basketball victories.)

- Make copies of the newspaper article "Cherry Creek Looks Shoplifting in the Face." After youngsters have read this, encourage them to discuss why kids shoplift. What ways can they brainstorm to stop shoplifting? How do they think honesty can be fostered and rewarded?

Cherry Creek looks shoplifting in the face

(Rocky Mountain News, Denver, Colorado, 12-25-92, p. 166)

By David Silverstain, Cherry Creek High School

Shoplifting has become an increasing problem for American merchants and a recent survey of Cherry Creek High School students produced some alarming results about this widespread crime.

Eight out of 10 people surveyed said that they had been with someone who shoplifted; three out of four said they had shoplifted before; less than two out of 10 had ever been caught.

The majority of students surveyed claimed to have shoplifted in the range of two to five times. The most common items stolen were priced between $2 and $5. The largest percentage of students surveyed said that they shoplifted because of peer pressure or just for the excitement of getting away with a crime.

Students surveyed were split over the question of whether they ever felt guilty about shoplifting. Many who had been pressured into it felt guilty, but those who did it for excitement felt little guilt. Many students said unorganized stores make for ideal shoplifting targets.

Although these results could be expected from any high school nationwide, they were nonetheless startling. This, combined with the fact that retailers lose nearly $5.1 billion each year due to shoplifting, and that each family in Colorado must spend $550 per year in the form of higher prices to make up for the losses incurred by merchants pushed a group of Cherry Creek High School students to design and implement an anti-shoplifting program.

Using the slogan, "Lift at the Gym, Not at the Mall," the program's goal is to prevent shoplifting and educate people on the harm of shoplifting.

The program hopes to educate students throughout the community by holding assemblies at West Middle School and Cherry Creek High School sending the message that shoplifting is not a cool thing to do; it's just plain stupid.

Students should know that all it takes to be guilty of shoplifting is to be an assistant to someone who conceals an item. Eventually, every shoplifter will be caught. Being caught is not exciting, it's embarrassing. And the embarrassment continues throughout the prosecution. Not only can civil fines of $150 be levied, but personal reputations can be ruined, and opportunities can be lost, now, and in the future.

Through the use of reverse peer-pressure, the students involved in this program hope to show other students that shoplifting is something that affects them personally and that it is best to stay away from the complications that shoplifting can create.

The campaign also hopes to deter shoplifters by placing information booths in area malls, where shoppers can register for free health club passes in exchange for pledging to help stop shoplifting. Other tactics used in the campaign include distributing anti-shoplifting promotional items to mall shoppers and merchants, proclaiming Dec. 19-26 as "Lift at the Gym, Not at the Mall" week in Greenwood Village, gaining publicity for the project through the media and enlisting the support of Gov. Roy Romer.

The program is being sponsored by Tamarac Square and King Soopers, in association with the Cherry Creek chapter of DECA, a marketing class and club. DECA is an organization of marketing students who learn skills taught in the classroom, and then are able to apply these skills at various competitions and in the implementation of projects that benefit the community. This public relations campaign will compete at the State DECA Conference in February.

Bibliography

Alexander, Martha. *We're in Big Trouble Blackboard Bear.* New York: Dial, 1980.

A small boy draws pictures of a bear on a blackboard, and when he steps right down, the trouble begins.

Avi. *Man from the Sky.* New York: Knopf, 1980.

Eleven-year-old Jamie spots a thief parachuting from an airplane.

Collier, James Lincoln. *Give Dad My Best.* New York: Four Winds Press, 1976.

Fourteen-year-old Jack Lundquist resorts to stealing kickback money during the Great Depression. The theft does not solve his real problem—his father's avoidance of responsibility.

Dahl, Roald. *Danny: The Champion of the World.* Illustrated by Jill Bennett. New York: Knopf, 1975.

Nine-year-old Danny lives in a Gypsy wagon in England with his father. Danny becomes a distinguished pheasant poacher.

Fleischman, Sid. *The Whipping Boy.* New York: Greenwillow, 1986.

Prince Brat and his whipping boy find their roles reversed and become involved with robbers and outlaws.

Mohr, Nicholasa. *In Nueva York.* New York: Dial, 1977.

A collection of short stories about daily life in a poor ethnic neighborhood. For mature readers.

Nixon, Joan Lowery. *The Orphan Train Quartet: A Family Apart.* New York: Bantam, 1987.

Mike's father has died, leaving his mother to support six children. During the 1860s the Kelly family is in dire poverty. Mike, age 11, turns to stealing to provide for his family, but he is caught. In order to keep Mike out of prison, Mrs. Kelly negotiates for all the children to be placed in new homes. And that is how they become part of the orphan-train saga and go to live with a variety of farm families in Missouri.

Paterson, Katherine. *The Great Gilly Hopkins.* New York: Thomas Y. Crowell, 1978.

There are few books that involve a child being caught in a theft. One of the best for starting discussions that involve a child stealing and being caught is *The Great Gilly Hopkins.* Gilly has been in three foster homes in three years. What is noteworthy about this book is the gradual and believable change in Gilly's behavior and character. This well-written, contemporary story takes readers inside Gilly's character and helps them understand the causes of her behavior. It can also take them outside themselves to reflect on their own behavior.

Platt, Kin. *Run for Your Life.* Photographs by Chuck Freedman. New York: Watts, 1977.

Fifteen-year-old Lee works to help his mother and is a track-team member. He discovers who has been stealing from the newspaper boxes on his route, and a story of morals and sports develops.

Rockwell, Thomas. *The Thief.* Illustrations by Gail Rockwell. New York: Delacorte, 1977.

Nine-year-old Tim is involved with his friend Dwayne in stealing and vandalism. This is a story of how a friendless boy wants companionship so badly that he lets himself be used.

Ungerer, Tomi. *The Three Robbers.* New York: Atheneum, 1962.

Three robbers who terrify the countryside are subdued by the charm of a little girl named Tiffany.

Being Suspected of Lying

The Liar's Contest

(from an African folktale)

One hot, hot day on the plains of Africa a fly, moth, and mosquito were out hunting. They happened upon Anansi the spider who was out strolling in the tall grass. These three flying hunters signaled to one another, "Let's get Anansi," and they swooped down on him. "What a tasty meal he will be," whined the mosquito.

The problem, though, was that all three together were not able to conquer him. On the other hand, Anansi was not able to beat them, so they struggled. After quite a long struggle, all four of them were exhausted and no one was a winner. "Why did you attack me?" asked Anansi.

The fly, moth, and mosquito, sitting on a plant leaf answered: "We were hungry. We were all out hunting, and because all living creatures must eat, we intended to eat you."

"Well, you were not able to beat me, and so you will never be able to eat me. Why should I not eat you three?" gasped Anansi.

"Ha! You were not able to get the best of us. How could you eat us?" they asked in a chorus.

"I have an idea," Anansi said with a chuckle. "Why don't we have a lying contest, and the winner gets to eat the loser." The three flying friends agreed.

Anansi decided to establish the rules for the contest: "Here is how we will do it. Each of us will tell an outrageous story. If I tell you that your stories are lies, you can eat me. If you tell me my story is a lie, I get to eat you."

The moth started his story first. "One day four days before I was born, my father was clearing new ground for

113

a garden with his sharp bush knife. He cut his foot with the knife and had to be carried to his bed. Well, I got us finished clearing the ground, plowed, planted, and tended the seed and harvested the crop. Four days later when I was born, my father was already a rich man."

Anansi curled himself up into a ball and thought about the moth's story. The fly, moth, and mosquito giggled as they waited for his answer. Finally, Anansi said, "How true. How true. How amazingly true." Now the three friends were surprised. They did not expect Anansi to give that answer, so they were forced to continue the contest.

Mosquito flitted around until he found the perfect place on the leaf to settle down and tell his story. "One time when I was hunting," he said, "I killed and ate an elephant. After such a big meal, I lay down in a clearing to play with the elephant's ear. A leopard came walking by, and because I was no longer hungry, I decided to play with the leopard. I chased him, caught him, grabbed him by the neck, shoved my fine fist down his throat, grabbed his tail from the inside, and pulled him inside out. The leopard had just eaten a sheep, and now the sheep was on the outside and the leopard was on the inside. The grateful sheep thanked me and went off munching and grazing into the grass."

Anansi untangled his legs, stretched, pondered, and said: "How true. How true. How amazingly true." Once more the three friends did not expect Anansi to give this answer. In fact, fly, moth, and mosquito were startled with Anansi's answer. And so, fly told his story: "There I was out hunting, and I saw a fat antelope. I slowly raised my gun, took aim, squeezed the trigger, and shot at the antelope. Then I ran forward, caught the antelope by the neck, killed it, and skinned and quartered it, and then my bullet came flying by. I caught the bullet and replaced it in my gun. Because I was quite hungry after all of this excitement and wanted to eat my catch alone, I climbed a tree with the meat, built a fire, cooked the meat, and ate it all. When

I was finished, I was so full that I could not climb down from the tree. Do you know that I had to go home to my village, get a rope, come back, and tie it to a limb of the tree to let myself down?"

Anansi turned himself around in several circles, cleaned all of his legs, and finally said: "How true. How true. How amazingly true." Again the three flying creatures did not know what to make of Anansi's answer. So now it was time for Anansi to take his turn in the contest.

"One day I was walking through the forest when I came upon a coconut lying in the path," said Anansi. "I picked up the coconut and called out to see if anyone could hear. 'I have just found a coconut,' I shouted. 'If no one comes to claim it, it is mine.' No one claimed it, so I took it home, planted, watered, and tended it. It grew. At last when it was a mature coconut tree with coconuts of its own, I climbed the tree and cut down three ripe coconuts. Then I cut each coconut open with my bush knife. When I cut open the first coconut, a fly flew out. When I cut open the second one, a moth fluttered out. When I cut open the third coconut, a mosquito buzzed out. Because the coconut belonged to me, the tree that grew from the coconut belonged to me. And because the tree belonged to me, the coconuts that grew on the tree belonged to me. And because the coconuts that grew on the tree belonged to me, the contents of the coconuts also belonged to me. So the fly, the moth, and the mosquito belonged to me. Because they belonged to me, I could do with them whatever I pleased. And I pleased to eat them. However, when I tried to eat them, they ran away. I have been looking for them ever since. And at last here they are—my fly, my moth, and my mosquito."

Fly, moth, and mosquito were speechless. They each wanted to say "How true," but they couldn't because that would admit that they were Anansi's property. Then it would naturally follow that he would eat the three of them. They couldn't say, "That is a lie!" because they would then lose the contest, and Anansi would eat them. They took the only possible course of action: They ran off into the forest. And that is why, to this very day, when spiders go hunting, they hunt for flies, moths, and mosquitoes. And when they catch them, they eat them—crunch, crunch, crunch. And the reason is that flies, moths, and mosquitoes belong to spiders because spider won the liar's contest. "How true. How true. How amazingly true!"

Discussion

Cultures throughout the world value truth. Universally, lying is considered evil and damaging. When someone is suspected of lying and even accused of it, it is a very hurtful experience. One of our sons was accused by his teacher of not writing the essay he turned in. She told him it was too good for him to be able to do at his age. Naturally, he never wrote anything that good for her again, and he has never forgotten that hurt.

There are gradations of lying. They include "little white lies" as when someone calls on the telephone for a family member, and you tell them that person is not home—at the family member's request. There are more deceitful outright lies, such as when you deny having done something such as breaking a plate, hitting your brother or sister, or getting all of your homework done.

When someone lies, they are being deceitful because their aim is generally to take advantage of someone. It is common that when someone gets the reputation of being a liar, people do not believe them even when they are telling the truth. Aesop's "The Boy Who Cried Wolf" is a clear example of that. It is said that liars must have good memories or they will get caught up in their lies.

Yet there are "liars" who are recognized as telling untruths out of sheer imaginativeness and clever amusement. Their tall tales are not harmful but are meant to be entertaining. Children and adults sometimes use exaggeration and playful inventions just for the fun of it—no malice intended.

When children tell a whooper, as parents and teachers we should not jump on them and accuse them of lying. Instead we might comment: "That was a very clever and funny tall tale. You really invented a great one!" We must make sure they know the difference between lying and distorting the truth as opposed to playing with language and thoughts and creating something that is different and colorful.

Activities

- Ask the youngsters to share about a time when they were caught telling a lie. What happened to them? How did they feel?

- Ask the children to tell you what they think the difference is between lying and telling tall stories.

- Has anyone ever told a lie to them? What did that lie make them feel like?

- After telling youngsters (or reading to them) "The Liar's Contest," organize a similar contest for them to take part in. Assemble a panel of three judges (to avoid a tie vote), and establish as many categories of winning stories as possible. Such categories might include the silliest, most unique, saddest, most surprising, shortest, and longest. Be prepared with a story of your own.

- Suggest that they might read some other stories about playing with ideas to amuse others.

- They might want to develop one of these stories into a readers' theater script or some creative dramatic activities.

Bibliography

Anno, Mitsumasa. "The Boy Who Cried Wolf." In *Anno's Aesop*, 32-34. New York: Orchard Books, 1989.
This story emphasizes the dangers of lying and shows that you cannot believe a liar even when the liar is telling the truth.

Ausubel, Nathan, ed. *A Treasury of Jewish Folklore*. New York: Crown, 1989.
Refer to the section "Liars and Braggarts" (pages 374-77). There are six playful stories that can be enjoyed and discussed.

Belloc, Hilaire. *Matilda Who Told Lies*. Illustrations by Steven Kellogg. New York: Dial, 1992.
Matilda could be the sister of the boy who cried wolf. This story has the same consequence: No one believes her even when she is telling the truth.

Chaikin, Miriam. *Lower! Higher! You're a Liar!* Illustrations by Richard Egielski. New York: Harper & Row, 1984.
The neighborhood bully taunts 10-year-old Molly and her friends. This story is set in Brooklyn at the time of World War II.

Gilson, Jamie. *You Cheat!* Illustrations by Maxie Chambliss. New York: Bradbury Press, 1992.
   Are cheating and lying the same thing? This humorous story about two little boys playing games and fishing really fits tall telling. After all, more tall tales are told about fishing than about almost anything else!

Schram, Peninnah. *Jewish Stories One Generation Tells Another*. Northvale, N.J.: Jason Aronson, 1987.
   This collection includes "The Seven Lies" (pages 328-34)—another example of a liar's contest.

Schwartz, Alvin. *Flapdoodle: Pure Nonsense from American Folklore*. New York: Lippincott, 1980.
   Schwartz has collected and retold stories that are just what the title of the book indicates.

_____. *Kickle Snifters and Other Fearsome Critters*. New York: Lippincott, 1976.
   Outlandish tall tales.

_____. *Tales of Trickery from the Land of Spoof*. New York: Farrar, Straus and Giroux, 1985.
   This is a collection of American trickster lore.

_____. *Tomfoolery: Trickery and Foolery with Words*. New York: Lippincott, 1973.
   Schwartz has put together a collection of delightful tomfoolery.

_____. *Whoppers: Tall Tales and Other Lies*. New York: Lippincott, 1975.
   The title tells it all!

Williams, Barbara. *Albert's Toothache*. Illustrations by Kay Chorao. New York: Dutton, 1974.
   This is the classic story of nobody believing Albert when he complains of a toothache. It helps to know that Albert is a turtle. It is really a terrible day until Albert's grandmother knows just the right question to ask.

Yolen, Jane, ed. *Favorite Folktales from Around the World*. New York: Pantheon, 1986.
   This anthology contains two stories about lying. They are "Helping to Lie" (page 27), and "The Ash Lad Who Made the Princess Say 'You're a Liar!' " (pages 28-29).

Eric and the Hospital
(from Norma Livo's personal family experience)

Five-year-old Eric had been running high fevers, but every time his mother got him in to see the doctor, the fever had dropped. "Regardless of when he gets another fever, call me immediately," Dr. Chesko told Eric's mom.

The very next Sunday morning Eric's fever shot up. Mother called the doctor, and he was contacted while in the hospital on his hospital rounds. "Bring him right up to the hospital. I want to see him now" was the order.

So Eric, his parents, his older sister, twin brother, and his younger brother all got into the family station wagon for the trip to the hospital. Eric was taken to the emergency room, and Dr. Chesko was paged. He arrived quickly, examined Eric, and told the nurses that Eric should be taken to a hospital room—he would be staying.

No one was prepared for this, especially Eric. His parents did not have time to get him ready for a hospital stay, and it was hard to communicate together since Dad stayed with the other kids in the waiting room. At that time the hospital policy was that kids under 10 years of age were not allowed in the hospital.

The three older kids were frightened when they heard that Eric would be staying, but their fear was nothing compared to Eric's. "Why do I have to get into the hospital bed?" "Where are they taking my clothes?" were his puzzled questions. "I don't like this thing" was his reaction to the hospital gown that opened in the back.

Then there was a parade of nurses taking his temperature, his blood pressure, and his blood. Oh yes, taking his blood. Eric screamed when the needles were used. Fear and terror were in his eyes. Mother tried to calm him and explain that the blood was needed for tests to find out what was making him sick.

"Okay, now, what's going on?" inquired Dr. Chesko when he came back. He poked Eric's stomach, checked his throat, and made doctor sounds of "ummmmmmmm." No words or comments, just a bunch of "ummmmmmmms."

Dad and the other kids went back home because there was nothing they could do there, but Eric's brothers and sister were horrified that they would be leaving Eric in this strange place. After several hours of tests and "ummmmmmmms" Eric became really upset. Now, Eric was a blankie boy. He loved his blankie, and right now he needed it. Mother phoned home and asked Dad to wash and dry the beloved blankie and bring it up to the hospital.

When the rather well-loved, tattered blankie arrived, the nurse in Eric's room snatched it away. "We cannot have that thing here," she ordered. Eric's eyes grew huge, and tears started to slide out of them and down his cheeks.

When Eric's mom kissed him good night when the announcement came that all visitors must leave and the nurse came in to verify that order, Eric looked so small in his bed.

It was a long night, but morning came, and the next day Dad stayed home from work so that Mom could go up to the hospital. The nurses greeted Mom quite coldly when she came into Eric's room. It did not take long to find out why. Dr. Chesko came in and laughed when he patted Eric. "You really fooled everyone, you possum," he said.

Then the doctor explained to Eric's mother that when the nurses came in to poke and prod him in the morning, Eric did not react. He just lay there. They called in another nurse, and then the same thing. They then sent out a call for Dr. Chesko who arrived, looked at Eric, and whispered in his ear: "Okay, possum. Wake up!" Eric had not fooled the doctor, but when the nurses saw Eric open his eyes to smile at the doctor, they were furious.

The diagnosis finally came that Eric had a case of blood poisoning. Dr. Chesko said it would have to be treated and that after it cleared up Eric would have to have his tonsils and adenoids removed, because they were the cause of the infection.

That afternoon Dad brought the other children up to the hospital, and Mother took Eric to the window in his room so that he could look outside and see his brothers and sister below. It was just as important for the kids to see Eric waving to them as it was for Eric to see them. They were not sure what was happening to him and needed to be reassured themselves.

Eric went home after two more days, and then two weeks later he went back to the hospital to get his tonsils and adenoids operated on.

They brought Eric out of the operating room with cuts and tears at both sides of his mouth. "He really fought going under," reported Dr. Chesko. "All he wanted to do was to go home." As Eric came out of the anesthetic in his hospital room he had to be held in bed by his mother. He reared up and demanded to go home. Mother insisted on staying with him that night—against hospital rules—and sat in his room holding his hand. The next morning the nurses ran more tests, and then they got Eric dressed. They changed the sheets on his bed and had him sitting on his suitcase waiting for the doctor to come in and sign him out. After one hour went by, Mother went out to the nurses' station and told them she was taking Eric home and that she would explain it all to Dr. Chesko. The nurses told her that that was not possible. "Eric must stay until the doctor comes," they said.

Mother just went back to Eric's room, took him by his hand, grabbed his suitcase, and started walking down the hall with the nurses yelling at her that she could not do that. "Obviously he is ready to go home," Mother told one of the nurses that caught up to her. "Enough is enough!"

As they walked out of the hospital Eric kept saying: "You are taking me home! You are taking me home! You are taking me home!"

"Yes indeed, Son, you are going home!" said his mom with a smile.

The doctor laughed when he talked with Mom. "You really made the nurses furious," he told her.

"Well, there was no reason for him to sit pitifully on his suitcase any longer," said Mom.

Eric's brothers and sister were so glad to have him home. They kept asking him about his operation and needed ice cream and ginger ale every time Eric did. However, after he was better, Mom and Dad noticed that every time they ate, Eric would ask, "Is this poison?" He asked this so many times that his brothers and sister soon began to take advantage of him. When there were treats handed out to all, they would tell Eric that it was poison. It was a long time before Eric stopped believing them and giving them his treats.

Discussion

This hospital story happened 35 years ago when practices in the hospitals were much different from those today. We now know that much more humane treatment helps patients in their recovery.

Today the medical profession uses puppets, tours, and make-believe to educate children before a hospital stay. Dentists put pictures up on their ceilings, use cassettes to soothe patients, and give out stickers after treatments.

Health and healing are natural subject matter in the study of religions. Healing by the laying on of hands, for example, created miracles such as the raising of Lazarus from the dead. There are many healing rituals. For us they are medicines, doctors, hospitals, clinics, and research. But religions from all cultures have used music, chanting, herbs, spices, unguents, and aromatics as well in healing practices. We refer to the operating "theater" and its spectacular setting, which can be compared to the shaman and their special rituals.

Stories and books about sickness and hospitalization are usually very clinical, informational, and didactic. We need to hear real stories of fears that we had as children and that children have today and to create our own stories about our fears and how we experienced and faced them. We need to remember. We need to create our personal stories of sickness and wellness. We also need to use creativity as a response to sickness.

Activities

- Ask the children to draw a picture of themselves being cured of an illness.

- Have the children write stories about illnesses they have had. Did it have a happy ending?

- Create with the children a song about getting well.

- Have the children put some sand in a tray and sculpt a representation of some bacteria or germ.

- Ask the children to use imagery to take someone sick through their sickness and along into the journey of getting well again. Imagine what this would be.

Bibliography

Duffy, James. *Doll Hospital.* New York: Scholastic, 1989.
    In this chapter book, Allison copes with her long-term illness through running a doll hospital.

Howe, James. *Night Without Stars.* New York: Atheneum, 1983.
    Donald helps Maria understand what will happen during her heart operation.

Jones, Rebecca C. *Angie and Me.* New York: Macmillan, 1981.
    Jenna learns from her roommate at the hospital that juvenile rheumatoid arthritis has changed her life.

Keller, Holly. *Best Present.* New York: Greenwillow, 1989.
    Young Rosie wants to visit her grandmother in the hospital.

Moyers, Bill. *Healing and the Mind.* New York: Doubleday, 1993.
    This book is directly related to the Public Affairs Television, Inc., and David Grubin Productions, Inc., television series "Healing and the Mind," presented by National Public Television during 1993.

Parabola. Society for the Study of Myth and Tradition, Inc., vol. 18, no. 1, February 1993.
This entire issue is devoted to the subject of healing. The society's address is 656 Broadway, New York, N.Y. 10012-2317.

Reit, Seymour. *Some Busy Hospital.* Illustrations by Carolyn Bracken. Chicago: Children's Press, 1985.
Describes activities in a hospital.

Rockwell, Anne, and Harlow Rockwell. *Emergency Room.* New York: Macmillan, 1985.
A young boy visits the emergency room for a sprained ankle.

Rogers, Fred. *Going to the Hospital.* Photographs by Jim Judkis. New York: Putnam, 1988.
Two children have brief hospital stays.

The Deserted Children

(from the Gros Ventre tribe of Montana)

One day a little boy and his sister, returning from play, found only smoldering campfires where their village had been. Deep in the distance the people could still be seen, traveling farther and farther away. As they hurried to catch up, the children found a tepee pole that had been dropped by their parents. "Mother!" they shouted. "Here is one of your poles!" But the parents were moving to a new camp and had left the children on purpose, not caring for them. From far away came the faint answer: "Never mind. You are not my child!"

The sister kept stopping to help her little brother, who was too young to keep going, and the two were soon left far behind. She led him to a thicket and, making him a bed of boughs, left him there to rest while she cut brush and built a small shelter. From then on they lived in this shelter, eating berries and roots gathered by the child-mother. Many summers passed. The children grew older.

One day as the girl was looking out of their little lodge, she saw a herd of elk going by, and she exclaimed: "Brother, look at the elk! So many!"

The boy was sitting with his head bowed. His eyes were cast downward, because he was then old enough to feel ashamed of living alone with his sister, and without looking up he replied, "Sister, it will do us no good if I look at them."

But she insisted. Then the boy raised his head and looked at the elk, and they all fell dead in their tracks.

The girl went out, skinned and butchered the elk, and carried the flesh and hides into the lodge. Looking at the pile of meat, she said, "I wish this meat were dried," and no sooner were the words out of her mouth than it was all perfectly dried. Lifting a hide and shaking it, she said, "I wish these hides were tanned," and so they were. She spread a number of them on the ground and murmured to herself, "I wish these were sewn into a tepee cover." Behold! There was a fine large tepee cover lying where the unsewn skins had been.

Later the same day a herd of buffalo appeared, and she cried: "Brother! Look at the buffalo!"

"Why do you want me to look at those buffalo?" he protested peevishly.

But she insisted, and when at last he raised his head, they too fell dead. Then she skinned them and brought the hides into the brush lodge, where she spread out a few and said, "I wish these hides were tanned into fine robes." Immediately they became what she wished. Then to the other skins she addressed the same magic words, and they became soft robes decorated with paintings. Now that she had everything she needed, she built and arranged her tepee.

One day the girl saw a raven flying by, and she called out: "Raven, take this piece of buffalo fat and go to the camp of my tribe. When you fly over, drop it in the center of the camp circle and say, 'There is plenty to eat at the old campsite!' "

The raven took the fat and flew to the faraway camp. There he saw all the young men playing the wheel game, and dropping his burden, he croaked, "There is plenty to eat at the old campsite!" It happened that at this time there was a famine in the village, and when the words of the raven were heard, the head chief ordered some young men to go to the old camp to see what they could find. The scouts set forth, and where the old camp had been they saw a fine elk-skin lodge with racks of meat swinging in the wind and buffalo grazing on the surrounding hills.

When the chief heard their report, he immediately told his crier to give the order to break camp.

When a new camp had been made near the elk-skin tepee, the father and the mother of the girl quickly discovered that it belonged to their daughter, and they went to her, calling: "My daughter! My daughter!" But she answered: "Keep back! You are not my father, and you are not my mother, for when I found the lodge poles and cried out to you not to leave me, you went on, saying that I was no daughter of yours!"

After a while, however, she seemed to forgive them, and calling all the people around her, she divided among them a large quantity of boiled buffalo tongues. She asked her parents to sit by her side. Meanwhile, her brother had been sitting with his head bowed.

Suddenly the girl cried: "Brother, look at these people! They are the ones who deserted us!"

She repeated her words twice, but the boy would not look up. At the fourth command he raised his head slowly, and as he looked around, the people fell lifeless.

Then the girl said: "Let a few of the men and women return to life so that the tribe may grow again, but let their characters be changed. Let the people be better than they were." Immediately some of them came to life, and the tribe increased, and their hearts were good.

(Reprinted with the permission of Four Winds Press, an imprint of Macmillan Publishing Company from *Girl Who Married a Ghost and Other Tales from North American Indians.*)

Discussion

Children fear being lost and separated from their parents from the time they are still babies and their parents leave them with baby-sitters, pre-school centers, or other family members. This fear of being lost can, like the Gros Ventre story, take on potent proportions. Did the parents really abandon them forever? If so, how can I, the child, get even with them?

Life has a way of offering many not-so-funny situations to children such as the frequently written news stories about parents leaving children—accidentally—at rest stops along the highway. Recently in the news, in fact, was the story of a family traveling along an interstate highway in Colorado who left their four-year-old son at a roadside stop when they all stopped for a break. All the adults in the car assumed that one of the other adults had made sure all the children were in the car. The four-year-old was picked up along the road by a truck driver who radioed to the state police. The parents had discovered the child missing, stopped at a telephone, and contacted 911. The family was joyously reunited. The child had actually gone to the car and was trying to get in when the mother drove off. Is this much different to the child from the experience of the sister and brother when the tribe left them behind?

In the same day's newspaper there was another story that demonstrates a modern cruel example of the fear of being lost. The headlines tell the problem: Parents Abandon Kids at N.J. Casinos. In the following Associated Press article are stories told by security guards about children who are left outside casinos unattended for hours at a time, at all times of the day and night. It would seem that some parents are not concerned with the security and safety of their children when engaged in gambling.

Newspapers are sometimes called literature in a hurry because all the stuff of the story is there, just in short form. The following three articles are good examples of literature in a hurry.

Trucker finds boy, 4, forgotten by family during 'potty break'

(Rocky Mountain News, Denver, Colorado, November 16, 1992, p.12)

By Natalie Soto, Rocky Mountain News Staff Writer

Mom reunited with tot she had left along I-25

A 4-year-old boy mistakenly left on the side of Interstate 25 when his family stopped for a "potty break" Sunday night was reunited with his distraught mother after a trucker stopped to pick him up.

The Fort Collins family—whose names were not available—decided to pull off northbound I-25 24 miles south of Colorado Springs, said State Patrol communications supervisor Gordon Sellin.

The mother wanted to settle down her fussy 1-year-old boy and give his 4- and 6-year-old brothers a chance to go to the bathroom, Sellin said.

She put the 6-year-old back in the car and thought the kids' teenage uncle had put the 4-year-old in also.

"He said that he tried to get the door open but 'Mommy drove off,'" Sellin said.

Thirty-two miles later, when she stopped at a gas station, she realized her middle son was missing.

Panicking, she called 911, which then called State Patrol.

Shortly before her call, someone else called to report that a trucker had picked up a small child from the highway. Sellin dispatched a trooper, who found the trucker and boy about halfway between the two spots.

The boy was found safe with a truck driver, who name also was unavailable, and then taken to the State Patrol office in Colorado Springs.

"The little guy said, 'Well, I was going to call the police, but there wasn't a phone,' " Sellin said with a chuckle.

"He was calm about it. He was in here playing with my computer keyboard until his mom came in."

Mom, however, was a little more panicked before she found her son, Sellin said.

"She was pretty upset," he said.

(Reprinted with permission of the *Rocky Mountain News*.)

Mother and 4-year-old tell how he came to be left on I-25

(*Rocky Mountain News*, Denver, Colorado, November 17, 1992, p.21)

By Natalie Soto, Rocky Mountain News Staff Writer

In his small 4-year-old voice, Craig Brucher told the story as best he could.

"I was going potty and Mommy left me," he said Monday night. "The police came and picked me up."

His mother, Jayme, tells the story a bit differently about how her little boy was left behind Sunday on Interstate 25 about 24 miles south of Colorado Springs.

"I always used to think, 'Come on. How could somebody leave their kid in a rest area?,'" she said. "But then that's what happened to me. I guess that's what I get for thinking that way."

Jayme Brucher, 30, was heading home to Fort Collins from Pueblo Sunday night with her three sons and 15-year-old brother when she pulled off the road to console her fussing 17-month-old, David.

Craig and his 6-year-old brother Michael left the car with their uncle for a "potty" break, she said.

She helped Michael into the driver's side "because I wanted to hold onto him since we were close to traffic," and yelled to her brother to help Craig into the car.

They drove off—just as Craig reached to open the door.

He told the two Texas truckers who picked him up, "'I need to call the police. My mommy's lost,'" Jayme Brucher said.

About 32 miles later, she stopped in Colorado Springs for gas and realized her middle child was missing.

"All I remember saying was, 'Oh my God' and 'He's just a baby.' I was panicked. I wanted to drive back and try and find him."

They were reunited a short time later at the Colorado State Patrol office in Colorado Springs.

Crying, she remembers the first words he spoke when he saw her.

"He just said, 'Didn't you hear me calling, Mommy? Did you miss me?' "

When they got home, Craig slept with Mom. "I knew exactly where he was," she said.

(Reprinted with permission of the *Rocky Mountain News*.)

Parents abandon kids at N.J. casinos

(*Rocky Mountain News*, Denver, Colorado, 11-16-92, p. 32)

Associated Press

Atlantic City, N.J.—Melissa leans against a casino wall, looking crumpled, tired and scared. She is 9 years old.

A few feet away, coins fall from slots into tin trays as red lights flash and bells ring. Dealers with magicians' hands slide chips and money across green felt tables. Cocktail waitresses in skimpy skirts, low-cut blouses and push-up bras serve free liquor to gamblers plopping down $100 bills.

It is midnight on a recent Friday at the Trump Taj Mahal. Melissa is waiting for her mother to finish gambling.

She has been here two hours, says a security guard. He is keeping an eye on Melissa while trying to locate her mom.

"My mother's in there and I want her," the little girl says, her brown eyes welling with tears. "I want to go to our room."

Melissa is one of scores of "casino kids," some as young as 6 months, whom workers say are left by their parents at the edge of gaming halls for hours at a time.

There is a law against leaving children unattended, said Winnie Comfort, a spokeswoman for the Department of Human Services. Parents who abandon their children face civil and criminal penalties, which vary depending on the nature of the offense. Anyone who fails to report an incident of possible child neglect or abuse can be charged with disorderly conduct.

But Comfort said the department's Division of Youth and Family Services does not get an unusually high number of complaints about children left at casinos, and does not keep separate statistics on them.

"On a scale from 1 to 10, the problem is a 10," said Susan Raff, a Taj Mahal security worker. "They should have a special place for children to go, manned 24 hours."

Executives at Harrah's, Bally's Park Place, Bally's Grand, Claridge, Merv Griffin's Resorts and the Showboat acknowledge the problem, but class it as negligible.

Trump Plaza and the Taj Mahal executives did not return telephone calls for comment, but officials at the Sands, Caesars, TropWorld and Trump Castle said they've never seen children abandoned at their establishments.

Yet in interviews over the last two months, workers at all of the city's 12 casinos told stories of parents who left infants in carriages or parked their youngsters on carpeted steps for long stretches, stopping back every few hours to check on them.

Vivian Robinson, a retired Philadelphia schoolteacher now employed at Resorts, said she once stopped a woman from hitting her child after the boy had her paged because he was hungry.

Atlantic City police Capt. Carlton Duncan said he remembered a man who had to be physically removed from the casino floor to get his children.

Late one night at Resorts not too long ago, 6-year-old Sharde spend hours waiting for her parents to come off the floor. Meanwhile, two fights broke out, and a woman passed out nearby. A man who appeared drunk walked over to Sharde and said, "What a pretty little girl."

When the girl's mother returned, she insisted to a reporter that she had left Sharde only "for a few minutes." She said she didn't think it unsafe because there were so many security guards around.

All gaming halls offer arcades and tout swimming pools and outdoor activities for people under 21, who by law aren't allowed in the casinos.

TropWorld has an amusement park with a $9.95 admission charge. Harrah's Marina has a state-licensed nursery providing child care for hotel guests free of charge. It is open until 10 p.m. daily during the summer, with reduced hours off-season, casino spokeswoman Alyce Parker said.

The other 11 casinos don't offer organized child care, though some provide referrals to baby-sitters.

Back at the Taj Mahal, supervisor Rose Ann Suydam kneels in front of Melissa and asks her to describe her mother. The girl fidgets with the string on her balloon and complains that she doesn't like coming to casinos.

Two pages go unanswered and Melissa starts crying harder. A 7-year-old friend of Melissa's warns that her mother will be angry about being paged.

Suydam and the night security manager, James Tirimacco, take Melissa to another part of the casino; they will not say how long it took to find her mother.

(Reprinted with permission of the *Rocky Mountain News*.)

Activities

- Read the two stories about the child being left by the family following a potty break. What information was left out of the first article? What questions do you still have even after reading both articles?

- Look in the daily newspaper for stories such as the three articles included in the discussion about lost or abandoned children. Develop one of them into a story to tell or a story to include in a class book of stories on lost children.

- Ask children if they can remember a time when they were lost? Where were they and what happened?

- Inquire whether the children have ever seen a lost child in a grocery store or shopping center. What did people who were nearby do? Did they help the child?

- Ask the children what families can do to avoid losing children in a crowd. Our family developed a family whistle that was used for rescues. List other ways to avoid losing each other.

- Schools go on many field trips. Have you ever heard of any children being lost on field trips? List the different ways teachers organize children so that no one will be left behind.

- Ask the children to interview a parent or a teacher to find out if they have ever had a lost-child experience.

- Encourage older children to go to a preschool or primary-grade classroom and to interview children to collect stories about lost children. These stories could be compiled into a book and shared with the children interviewed.

Bibliography

Bierhorst, John, ed. *Girl Who Married a Ghost and Other Tales from North American Indians.* Photographs by Edward S. Curtis. New York: Macmillan, 1978.

Bograd, Larry. *Lost in the Store.* Illustrations by Victoria Chess. New York: Macmillan, 1981.
    Bruno gets lost in a department store, but a friendly worker helps him.

Carrick, Carol. *The Foundling.* Illustrations by Donald Carrick. New York: Seabury Press, 1977.
    Christopher finds a lost dog that he adopts after his own dog has been killed.

_____. *The Highest Balloon of the Common.* New York; Greenwillow, 1977.
    Paul is lost during an old-fashioned county fair, but Father has devised a way to find him in just such an eventuality.

_____. *Left Behind.* Illustrations by Donald Carrick. New York: Clarion, 1988.
    Christopher and his partner get separated from others on a school field trip. Then follows the drama in everyday happenings.

_____. *Lost in the Storm.* Boston: Houghton Mifflin, 1974.
    A dog is lost overnight in a storm. Every child who has ever had a lost dog will have empathy for this dog.

Cohen, Miriam. *Lost in the Museum.* Illustrations by Lillian Hoban. New York: Greenwillow, 1978.
    Jim and his friends wander away from the group and get lost in the American Museum of Natural History.

Goble, Paul. *The Lost Children.* New York: Bradbury Press, 1993.
    This is a Blackfoot Indian legend in which six neglected orphaned brothers decide to go to the Above World where they become the constellation of the "Lost Children" or Pleiades. Goble expands on the theme through art and symbols.

Hines, Anna Grossnickle. *Don't Worry I'll Find You.* New York: Dutton, 1986.
    Sarah is out shopping at a mall with her mother and her doll, but she misplaces her doll and gets herself lost in the process.

Leigh, Bill. *The Far Side of Fear*. New York: Viking, 1977.

Thirteen-year-old Kenny and his friends become trapped in a cave. The adventure is told from multiple viewpoints.

Myers, Bernice. *A Lost Horse*. New York: Doubleday, 1975.

A horse that is lost in the city stands little chance of finding his way out without help. Young readers will empathize with the horse.

Parenteau, Shirley. *I'll Bet You Thought I Was Lost*. Illustrations by Lorna Tomei. New York: Lothrop, Lee & Shepard, 1981.

While out grocery shopping with Dad, little Sandy gets lost. The store aisles look longer, and the shopping carts and legs look familiar. A humorous and contemporary adventure.

Tompert, Ann. *Will You Come Back for Me?* Illustrations by Robin Kramer. Niles, Ill.: Albert Whitman, 1988.

Four-year-old Suki is worried about being left in day care for the first time until her mother reassures her that she loves her and will always return for her.

Weiss, Nicki. *Waiting*. New York: Greenwillow, 1981.

When you are very little, even a few minutes is a long time to wait for your mother to come back. Mama thinks Annalee does not even know she is gone, but Annalee knows better.

Norwegian Treasure

(retold by Norma J. Livo and based on the legend of King
Guntram that is widely known in Scandinavia)

Two young, blond, tall Norwegian fellows—Lars and
Eric—were traveling from Oslo to Trondheim to look for
work in the fjords above the Gaula River. It was the season
of the long days, when the sun barely set before it rose
again in the sky. As these companions walked they talked
of what they were going to do with all of the money they
would earn. They had thoughts of buying a boat, land and
clothes, and of finding wives and settling down to a life of
leisure. As they walked, their stomachs complained about
the lack of food.

"If I had money," said Lars, "I would buy us the largest
wheel of cheese in the shop, some fresh bread, and butter,
and we would fill our stomachs for a change."

"Ah," Eric said wistfully. "I would buy us some her-
ring and potatoes and pickles to add to your food."

Because the sun was bright both day and night, sleeping was done when they were exhausted from walking. At
one of their rest stops, they made soft places to sleep on
with the boughs of pine trees. They used their backpacks
for pillows. This particular time Lars woke up first. While
Eric slept, Lars noticed that Eric had a smile on his face.
Lars stretched and watched the birds of the forest flitting
and teasing the squirrels. He went over to the stream
nearby and scooped up water in his cupped hands and
splashed his face and neck. Playfully, he took another
scoop of water over to Eric and sprinkled it on Eric's face.
Eric woke up and, very unusual for him, yelled at Lars.

"Why did you wake me up?" Eric demanded. "I was just having a dream about a mouse that spoke to me and told me to find the richest person's home in Trondheim, go out to his backyard, find his herb garden, dig under the thyme, and there I would find gold."

"Calm down, Eric. I am sorry but I did not see any mice as you slept. Your dream is one that I wish I had. Such a dream. You have always been lucky," observed Lars.

They packed up and continued on their journey, but all either of them could think of was Eric's dream. "Do you think there could be any truth to your dream, Eric?" asked Lars.

"Why not?" answered Eric. "That mouse didn't look or sound like any ordinary mouse. He had strands of gold for his whiskers, and his eyes were two big emeralds. Does that sound like any mouse you have ever dreamed about—let alone seen?"

The closer they got to Trondheim the more certain they became that Eric's dream meant something special and that they should search for the richest person in town. They got to Trondheim late in the afternoon. They looked rumpled and had run out of the little money they had had between them. They faced the rest of the day without food. Once in town they decided they certainly had nothing to lose, so they started inquiring of the people they passed about where the richest person in town lived.

They heard one person named by five townspeople, so they figured that they would approach him about digging in his backyard. It was not hard to find the home of the richest person in Trondheim. It was rather obvious when they traveled through the elaborate gates and up the long road that led to a mansion. They straightened their hair as well as they could and dusted their clothes—neither act making too much difference in how they looked. They knocked on the huge grand door with carved griffins on it. A servant answered the door and Eric and Lars quite confidently asked for the owner of the house. With a quizzical look, the servant led them to a huge study with tables, books, and walls of walnut wood. After a short interval, a massive, florid-faced red-haired man came and introduced himself as the owner. His name was Karl.

Lars and Eric tumbled over each other's explanation about why they were there. They asked him if he had thyme planted in his garden. "Of course," Karl boomed.

They pleaded with him to let them go out and dig, and they promised him that they would share the gold with him. "You lads look tired and hungry," Karl declared. "Why not join me for supper and stay the night? In the morning I will have my servants dig to see if there is any truth to your dream."

Of course the travelers thought this was a grand idea and just the beginning of their new life of riches. They had agreed to share whatever they found with each other, so sharing a bit more with Karl and some servants seemed fair.

For supper that night they ate beef, chicken, fish, and fancy foods they did not even recognize. And when they climbed into beds with sheets and real pillows, they fell asleep instantly. Not so Karl. After supper he called to two of his servants. "Those two foolish fellows do not deserve riches from my property. Let's go out and dig it up our-selves tonight."

The sun gave them plenty of light as they dug in the herb garden. Karl sat on a big boulder and watched the men as they swung their shovels and scooped dirt out from under the thyme. Sure enough, there was a teak chest with bands of silver around it right under the thyme. The servants pulled it out of the hole, and it was heavy. Obvi-ously, it was filled with untold riches. Karl broke open the hasp and opened the lid. Just as it opened ever so slightly, something whisked by their heads and into the sky. When the lid was fully opened, all they could see was the inside of the teak chest. It was empty. There was nothing in it. They picked it up, and it was light and handled easily.

What a mystery! So Karl and the men put the chest back in the ground, covered it over with dirt, and replaced the thyme plants on top of that.

In the morning before breakfast or anything else, Lars and Eric insisted to Karl that they wanted first to find the treasure. Karl smirked and agreed. Outside in the garden, Karl pointed out the thyme part of the garden. There were fragrant flowers, delicate blooms, and several varieties of thyme. Lars and Eric each took a shovel, but in their eagerness they never noticed the fresh dirt left on the blades of the shovels. They dug carefully, took the thyme plants out and placed them on the side so that they could replant them after they had taken the treasure out. They dug through the earth, which was amazingly soft—little suspecting why this was so. And there their shovels hit the teak chest with silver bands around it. The top of the chest was carved, and they could see mice with gold whiskers and emerald eyes all over it. Greedy Karl had not even noticed this art last night. The lock on the hasp opened with their touch, and the two companions took a deep breath and lifted the lid. There inside was enough gold to make them the richest people in Trondheim and then some. They generously shared with Karl and his servants.

And so that is the way it is: If a greedy person tries to dig up a cask of gold, it will turn into an empty cask. But the people who are supposed to get the money, will amazingly get it. The riches as foretold by the dream mouse were only meant for the dreamer to find and not anyone else.

Lars and Eric had many pleasant dreams during the rest of their lives, and it seemed that they always learned something of value from each of their dreams.

Discussion

Not all dreams are scary. In fact, many cultures believe that dreams are the source of all wisdom. Some Native Americans have a tradition of weaving nets to protect their babies from harmful dreams. And they tell their children as they sleep to try to dream and remember what they dream. Scary dreams will be caught in the web, or dream catcher, so only the good dreams get through.

In Asian countries a replica of a mythological creature called the Bah Koo is placed by the bed of children. Its purpose: to gobble up the bad dreams.

Nightmares are universal, though. Children generally fear the frightening things that they frequently conjure up to complement their uncomfortable imaginings.

The fear children feel of having a scary dream is the fourteenth fear reported by children in Kaoru Yamamoto's study, "Voices in Unison," and yet children's literature is filled with books exploring this topic. Other higher-rated fears, such as urinating in class, are ignored. That does not mean that it is an imaginary fear, but probably it is not as frightening as adults think it might be.

Once when I was preparing to give a presentation on children's fears as seen in children's books, I had the dining-room table filled with books. Mercer Mayer's *There's a Nightmare in My Closet* was one of the books on top of the pile. My youngest son, Rob—6 feet 4 inches and a parent himself—saw the book. He picked it up and read it and then put it back on the table, saying, "That's just the way it was back in Tarentum, Mom."

I asked him what he was talking about, and then he told me something I had never known. "Do you remember that when you tucked me into bed at night, I always made sure you closed the closet door?" he asked. I did remember his asking me to close the closet door, but in retrospect I thought he was just getting neat and wanted the door closed. "No," he continued, "I had a monster that lived inside the closet. In fact, one night you did not close the closet door, and the next morning I woke up in the closet where the monster had taken me."

"Rob, why have you never told me about this before?" I demanded.

"Because I thought you knew" was his reply. Yes, he had had monsters in his closet and dreams about them, but they evidently had not troubled him too much.

We should emphasize the positive qualities of dreams in the way the Native American tradition does. We must also provide ways to reduce the fears of scary dreams. Of course, this notion applies to normal kids who do not have crippling psychological problems.

Activities

- Literature can give children the opportunity to talk about their fears. If they are responding to a book, encourage them to say how they feel and to put their fears in perspective.

- Refer to the books in the bibliography. There are many open-ended discussion questions that can be identified in them. Rob was a youngster in the era before *There's a Nightmare in My Closet.* Otherwise, it would have been easy to read this story to him, and maybe it would have provoked his telling me about his monster.

- Ask the children to think of what kind of things they could say to one of their friends that would prove that not all dreams are bad or scary.

- Have children make a list of big, scary, monstrous, nightmare words, and discuss why these words have that quality to them.

- Have children create other ways to ward off bad dreams such as the dream catcher or the Bah Koo. One family came up with the idea of using perfume or cologne in a spray bottle and spraying it in the room so that the monsters could not cross into it. The children could also write or tell stories about their special creations. Children are most successful when they find their own methods to deal with what they fear and when they are helped to experience their own frightening situations gradually.

- Ask what things you might do to alleviate fears and give reassurance when youngsters have bad dreams. Let them help solve the problem.

- Share some of your childhood nightmares. Children can be surprised to find out that adults have had such fears and still remember them and possibly still have them.

Bibliography

Apple, Margot. *Blanket.* Boston: Houghton Mifflin, 1990.
    The child cannot get to sleep because the bedtime blanket is hanging outside on the clothesline. The dog, the cat, the rest of the clothes, and the wind conspire to get it safely inside to its owner. A warm, charming bedtime story.

Babbitt, Natalie. *The Something*. New York: Dell, 1970.
Mylo, the little monster, sculpted what he was afraid of to show to his mother. The story includes sly humor as to what constitutes a nightmare monster. It all depends on your point of view.

Bilezikian, Gary. *While I Slept*. New York: Orchard Books, 1990.
Did night noises spook you as a youngster? This story of a little boy sleeping during a noisy night might remind you of some night noises you knew.

Calhoun, Mary. *While I Slept*. Illustrations by Ed Young. New York: Morrow, 1992.
A perfect book for sharing at bedtime because Mother and Father explain to their child where all the other creatures go to sleep.

Grifalconi, Ann. *Darkness and the Butterfly*. Boston: Little, Brown, 1987.
Little Osa is fearless during the day while climbing trees or exploring the African valley where she lives, but at night she becomes afraid of the strange and terrifying things that might lie in the dark.

Hennessy, B. G. *Sleep Tight*. Illustrations by Anthony Carnabuci. New York: Viking, 1992.
Two children see what a special place their house becomes as they are tucked into bed and everything around them is ready for sleep.

Howe, James. *There's a Monster Under My Bed*. Illustrations by David Rose. New York: Atheneum, 1986.
Simon is sure there are monsters under his bed in the night—he can even hear them breathing. Two brothers find nighttime comfort with each other.

Martin, Bill, Jr., and John Archambault. *The Ghost-Eye Tree*. Illustrations by Ted Rand. New York: Holt, Rinehart and Winston, 1985.
Any child who has been frightened of the dark will enjoy this book.

Mayer, Mercer. *There's an Alligator Under My Bed*. New York: Dial, 1987.
This is the sequel to *There's a Nightmare in My Closet*. The alligator under his bed makes a boy's bedtime a hazardous operation until he lures it out of the house and into the garage.

____. *There's a Nightmare in My Closet*. New York: Dial, 1968.
The classic nightmare story of a little boy who has a nightmare who lives in his closet. However, the nightmare turns out to be timid, cowardly, oversensitive, and a crybaby.

____. *There's Something in My Attic.* New York: Dial, 1988.
Still conquering nightmares, this time Mayer has as the main character a little girl who conquers the nightmare in the attic above her head.

McLerran, Alice. *Dreamsong.* Illustrations by Valery Vasiliev. New York: Tambourine Books, 1992.
A boy searches fields, forests, and mountains for the song he hears each night in his dream, unaware that the true source is in his own home.

Mossman, Barbara. *The Night Lion.* Illustrations by Werner Farber. Boston: Houghton Mifflin, 1991.
Laura has been put to bed but she cannot sleep. It's too dark. She can hear something rustling, and she is sure it is pirates. Her best toy, the Lion, promises to protect her, but she finds out that he is afraid of dragons. So they come to protect each other through the night.

Osofsky, Audrey. *Dreamcatcher.* Illustrations by Ed Young. New York: Orchard Books, 1992.
The Ojibwa Indians of the Great Lakes treasured good dreams as the source of all wisdom. They wove nets to protect their babies from harmful dreams, and children going to sleep were told to dream and to remember what they dreamed. A lovely book!

Rhodes, Robert V. *Bah Koo.* Illustrations by Gary Patterson. New York: St. Martin's Press, 1986.
This is based on an ancient legend of China and Japan. The magical creature that protects children as they sleep has the body and mane of a lion, is spotted like a leopard, has the ears of a cow, a nose like an elephant's trunk, and four claws on each of its feet. It has powerful fangs that can chew through the hardest of objects. Its single prey is bad dreams: It gobbles them up. This is an updated version of the Bah Koo.

Sendak, Maurice. *Where the Wild Things Are.* New York: Harper, 1963.
The dream story that is the ultimate classic. Max has been a monster all day, and in his dreams he goes off to the land where the wild things are and becomes their leader. He returns home and finds his mother still loves him.

Shepperson, Rob. *The Sandman.* New York: Farrar, Straus and Giroux, 1989.
This story involves another nighttime mythology—the sandman. Instead of going to sleep one night Jay decides to see if the sandman will really come and sprinkle sand on his eyes. His night is filled with a wheelbarrow of magic.

Van Allsburg, Chris. *Just a Dream.* Boston: Houghton Mifflin, 1990.
    The nightmare of pollution is Walter's dream. He has a dream about a future Earth devastated by pollution and begins to recognize the importance of taking care of the environment.

Willis, Jeanne. *The Monster Bed.* Illustrations by Susan Varley. New York: Lothrop, Lee & Shepard, 1986.
    A little monster is afraid to go to bed because he thinks humans will get him while he is asleep. The artist received permission for the use of the characters from the all-time dream classic, *Where the Wild Things Are* by Maurice Sendak.

Yamamoto, Kaoru, Abdalla Soliman, James Parsons, and O. L. Davies, Jr. "Voices in Unison: Stressful Events in the Lives of Children in Six Countries." *Journal of Child Psychology and Psychiatry* 28, no. 6 (1987): 855-64.

The Singing Bone
(collected by Jacob Grimm and Wilhelm Grimm)

A wild boar terrorized a certain country as it attacked workers in the fields, killed men, and tore them to pieces with its terrible tusks. The king of the country had offered rich rewards to any one who would rid the land of this monster. But no man could even be persuaded to enter the forest where the animal made its home, because the beast was so huge and ferocious.

In desperation the king proclaimed that he would give his only daughter in marriage to any man who would bring the wild boar to him dead or alive.

Two brothers lived in this country. They were the sons of a poor man. They gave notice that they would enter into this perilous undertaking. The elder, who was clever and crafty, was influenced by pride. The younger brother was innocent and simple and offered himself from the kindness of his heart.

The king advised them that the best and safest way would be to take opposite directions in the wood. The elder brother was to go in the evening, the younger in the morning.

The younger brother had not gone far when a little fairy stepped up to him. The fairy held in his hand a black spear and said: "I will give you this spear, because your heart is innocent and good. With this you can go out and discover the wild boar, and he shall not be able to harm you."

He thanked the little man, took the spear, placed it on his shoulder, and without delay he went farther into the forest. It was not long before he saw the animal coming toward him all ready to spring on him. The youth stood still and held the spear firmly in front of him. In a wild rage, the fierce beast ran violently toward him and was met by the spear. It seemed that the boar threw himself on the point, and as it pierced his heart, the animal fell dead.

The younger brother took the dead monster on his shoulder and took off to find his brother. As he approached the other side of the wood, he saw a large hall and heard music. He found a number of people dancing, drinking wine, and making merry. His elder brother was among them, because he thought the wild boar would not run far away, and he wished to gather up his courage for the evening by cheerful company and wine.

When he caught sight of his younger brother coming out of the forest laden with his booty, jealousy and malice rose in his heart. He disguised his bitter feelings and spoke kindly to his brother: "Come in and stay with us, dear brother, and rest a while. Get up your strength by a cup of wine."

Not suspecting that anything was wrong, the younger brother carried the dead boar into the hall. He told his brother of the little man he had met in the wood who had given him the spear. He described too how he had killed the vicious animal.

The older brother persuaded him to stay and rest till the evening, and then they went out together in the twilight and walked by the river till the night became quite dark. A little bridge lay across the river that they had to pass. The elder brother let the young one go before him. At the middle of the stream the wicked man gave his younger brother a blow from behind, and he fell down dead instantly.

Fearing he might not be quite dead, the older brother threw the body over the bridge into the river. Through the clear waters he saw it sink into the sand. After this wicked deed he ran home quickly, took the dead wild boar on his shoulders, and carried it to the king. He pretended that he had killed the animal, and, therefore, he claimed the princess as his wife according to the king's promise.

But dark deeds are not often concealed, for something usually happens to bring them to light. And so it was that not many years after, a herdsman passing over the bridge with his flock saw beneath him in the sand a little bone as white as snow. He thought it would make a nice mouthpiece for his horn. So as soon as the flock passed over the bridge he waded into the middle of the stream—for the water was very shallow—took up the bone, and carried it home.

He made a mouthpiece for his horn, but the first time he blew the horn after the bone was in it, it filled the herdsman with wonder and amazement, for it began to sing. These were the words it sang:

Ah! dear shepherd, you are blowing your horn
With one of my bones, which night and morn
Lie still unburied, beneath the wave
Where I was thrown in a sandy grave.
I killed the wild boar, and my brother slew me,
And gained the princess by pretending 'twas he.

"What a wonderful horn," said the shepherd. "It can sing of itself! I must certainly take it to my lord, the king."

As soon as the horn was brought before the king and blown by the shepherd it at once began to sing the same song and the same words. The king at first was surprised, but his suspicion was aroused. He ordered the sand under the bridge to be examined immediately. The entire skeleton of the murdered man was discovered, and the whole ghastly deed came to light.

The wicked brother could not deny the deed, however. And the king ordered him to be tied in a sack and drowned. But the remains of his murdered brother were carefully carried to the churchyard and laid to rest in a beautiful grave.

The Fisherman and His Wife

(collected by Jacob Grimm and Wilhelm Grimm)

There was once a fisherman and his wife who lived together in a hovel by the seashore. The fisherman went out every day with his hook and line to catch fish. He angled and angled. One day as he was sitting with his rod and looking into the clear water he felt the line go to the bottom. When he drew it up, he found a great flounder on the hook. The flounder spoke to him: "Fisherman, listen to me. Let me go. I am not a real fish but an enchanted prince. What good shall I be to you if you land me? I shall not taste well. Put me back into the water again, and let me swim away."

"Well," said the fisherman, "no need of so many words about the matter. Because you can speak, I had much rather let you swim away."

Saying this the fisherman put him back into the clear water, and the flounder sank to the bottom, leaving a long streak of blood behind him. The fisherman got up and went home to his wife in their hovel.

"Well, husband," said the wife. "Have you caught nothing today?"

"No," said the fisherman. "That is, I did catch a flounder, but as he said he was an enchanted prince, I let him go."

"Then did you not wish for something?" asked the wife.

"No," said the man. "What should I have wished for?"

"Oh dear!" said the wife. "It is so dreadful to always live in this evil-smelling hovel. You might as well have wished for a little cottage. Go again and call him. Tell him we want a little cottage. I daresay he will give it to us. Go and be quick."

When he went back, the sea was green and yellow and not nearly so clear. The fisherman stood and called:

O man, O man!—if man you be,
Or flounder, flounder, in the sea—
Such a tiresome wife I've got,
For she wants what I do not.

The flounder came swimming up and said, "Now then, what does she want?"

"Oh," answered the man, "you know, when I caught you, my wife says I ought to have wished for something. She does not want to live any longer in our hovel. She would rather have a cottage."

"Go home with you," said the flounder, "she has it already."

The man went home and found instead of the hovel a little cottage. His wife was sitting on a bench by the door. She took him by the hand and said to him, "Come in and see if this is not a great improvement."

They went in, and there was a little house place and a beautiful little bedroom, a kitchen and larder, all sorts of furniture, and iron and brass ware of the very best. At the back was a little yard with fowls and ducks and a little garden full of green vegetables and fruit.

"Look," said the wife, "is that not nice?"

"Yes," agreed the fisherman. "If this can only last, we shall be very well contented."

"We will see about that," answered his wife.

After a warm meal they went to bed. All went well for a week or fortnight when the wife said: "Look here husband. The cottage is really too confined, and the yard and garden are so small. I think the flounder had better get us a larger house. I should like very much to live in a large stone castle. Go to your fish, and he will send us a castle."

"Oh, my dear wife," said the man. "The cottage is good enough. What do we want a castle for?"

"We want one," whined the wife. "Go along with you. The flounder can give us one."

"Now, wife," said the fisherman, "the flounder gave us the cottage. I do not like to go to him again. He may be angry."

"Go along," insisted his wife. "He might just as well give us it as not. Do as I say!"

The fisherman felt very reluctant and unwilling. He said to himself, It is not the right thing to do. Nevertheless, he went.

When he came to the seaside, the water was purple and dark blue and gray and thick, not green and yellow as before. He stood and said:

O man, O man!—if man you be,
Or flounder, flounder, in the sea—
Such a tiresome wife I've got,
For she wants what I do not.

"Now then, what does she want?" asked the flounder as he came to the surface of the water.

"Oh," confided the man half frightened, "she wants to live in a large stone castle."

"Go home with you. She is already standing before the door," said the flounder.

The man went home, and when he got there, there stood in the place of the cottage a great castle of stone. His wife was standing on the steps about to go in. She took him by the hand and said, "Let us enter."

They went in, and in the castle was a great hall with a marble pavement. There were a great many servants who led them through large doors. The passages were decked with tapestries, and the rooms had golden chairs and tables. Crystal chandeliers hung from the ceiling, and all the rooms had carpets. The tables were covered with eatables and the best wine for any one who wanted them. At the back of the castle was a great stable yard for horses and cattle. The carriages were the finest. On the side there was a splendid large garden with the most beautiful flowers and fine fruit trees. There were forests with deer and oxen and sheep and everything that the heart could wish for.

"There!" exclaimed the wife. "Is this not beautiful?"

"Oh, yes," whispered the fisherman. "If it will only last, we can live in this fine castle and be very well contented."

"We will see about that," said his wife tartly. "In the meantime, we will sleep on it." With that, they went to their fine bed with a soft goose-feather mattress.

The next morning the wife woke up first, just at the break of day. She looked out and saw from her bed the beautiful country lying all round. The man took no notice of it, so she poked him in the side with her elbow and said: "Husband. Get up and just look out of the window. Look. Just think if we could be king over all this country! Just go to your fish and tell him we should like to be king."

"Now, wife," said the man. "What should we be king for? I could not ask him for such a thing."

"Why not?" asked his wife. "You must go directly. I insist. I must be king."

So the man went—very much put out that his wife should want to be king. It is not the right thing to do. Not at all the right thing, thought the man. He had not at all wanted to go, and yet he went all the same. When he came to the sea, the water was quite dark gray and rushed far inland and had an ill smell. He stood and called:

O man, O man!—if man you be,
Or flounder, flounder, in the sea—
Such a tiresome wife I've got,
For she wants what I do not.

"Now then, what does she want this time?" asked the fish.

"Oh dear!" said the fisherman. "She wants to be king."

"Go home with you, she is king already," announced the fish.

The fisherman went back, and as he came to the palace he saw it was very much larger and had great towers and splendid gateways. A herald stood before the massive door, and a number of soldiers were marching with kettledrums and trumpets.

Inside everything was of marble and gold. There were many heavy curtains with great golden tassels. He went through the doors of the salon to where the great throne room was, and there was his wife sitting upon a throne of gold and diamonds. She was wearing a great golden crown, and the scepter in her hand was of pure gold and jewels. On each side stood six pages in a row. Each one was a head shorter than the other. The fisherman went up to her and said: "Well, wife. Now you are king!"

"Yes," said the wife, "now I am king."

The fisherman stood and looked at her, and after he had gazed at her for some time, he marveled: "Well, wife. This is fine for you to be king! Now there is nothing more to wish for."

"Oh, husband!" snapped his wife, "I am tired of this already. Go to your fish and tell him that now that I am king I must be emperor."

"Now, wife," reasoned the fisherman. "What do you want to be emperor for?"

"Husband," ordered she, "go and tell the fish I want to be emperor."

"Oh dear!" moaned the man. "I cannot do it. I cannot ask him for such a thing. There is but one emperor at a time. The fish cannot possibly make anyone emperor. Indeed, he cannot."

"Now, look here," snarled the wife. "I am king, and you are only my husband, so will you go at once! Go along! If he was able to make me king, he is able to make me emperor. I will and must be emperor! Go along!"

The fisherman was obliged to go. As he went he felt very uncomfortable about it, and he thought to himself: It is not at all the right thing to do. To want to be emperor is really going too far. The flounder will soon be beginning to get tired of this.

He came to the sea, and the water was quite black and thick, and the foam flew, and the wind blew, and the man was terrified. But he stood and said:

O man, O man!—if man you be,
Or flounder, flounder, in the sea—
Such a tiresome wife I've got,
For she wants what I do not.

"What is it now?" asked the fish.

"Oh dear," said the fisherman. "My wife wants to be emperor."

"Go home with you," directed the fish. "She is emperor already."

The fisherman went home and found the castle adorned with polished marble and alabaster figures and golden gates. The troops were being marshaled before the door, and they were blowing trumpets and beating drums and cymbals. When he entered, he saw barons and earls and dukes waiting about like servants. The doors were all of bright gold. He saw his wife sitting upon a throne made of one entire piece of gold, and it seemed about 2 miles high. She was wearing a great golden crown that was about 3 yards high and set with brilliants and carbuncles. In one hand she held the scepter; in the other, the globe. On both sides of her stood pages in two rows, all arranged according to their size—from the most enormous giant of 2 miles high to the tiniest dwarf of the size of a little finger. Before her stood earls and dukes in crowds.

The fisherman went up to her and said: "Well, wife. Now you are emperor."

"Yes," she agreed. "Now I am emperor."

He went and sat down and had a good look at her, and then he said, "Well now, wife, there is nothing left to be. Now you are emperor."

"What are you talking about husband?" she asked. "I am emperor, and next I will be Pope! Go and tell the fish so."

"Oh dear," complained the man. "What is it that you do not want? You can never become Pope. There is but one Pope in Christendom, and the fish cannot possibly do it."

"Husband," she said curtly, "no more words about it. I must and will be Pope. So go along to the fish."

"Now, wife," said the fisherman. "How can I ask him such a thing? It is too bad. It is asking too much, and besides, he could not do it."

"That's rubbish," she said scornfully. "If he could make me emperor, he can make me Pope. Go along and ask him. I am emperor, and you are only my husband, so you must go."

This time as he went to the sea he felt very frightened. He shivered and shook, and his knees trembled. There rose a great wind, and the clouds flew by, and it grew very dark. The sea rose mountains high, and the ships were tossed about. The sky was partly blue in the middle, but at the sides it was very dark and red. It looked like a great tempest. He felt very despondent and stood trembling and said:

O man, O man!—if man you be,
Or flounder, flounder, in the sea—
Such a tiresome wife I've got,
For she wants what I do not.

"Well, what now?" asked the fish.
"Oh dear!" said the fisherman. "She wants to be Pope."
"Go home with you. She is Pope already," said the fish.

He went home, and he found himself standing before a great church with palaces all round. He had to make his way through a crowd of people. When he got inside, he found the place lighted up with thousands and thousands of lights. His wife was clothed in a golden garment and sat upon a very high throne. She had three golden crowns on, all in the greatest priestly pomp. On both sides of her there stood two rows of lights of all sizes—from the size of the longest tower to the smallest rushlight—and all the emperors and kings were kneeling before her and kissing her feet.

"Well, wife," said the man as he stared at her, "so you are Pope."

"Yes," she said, "now I am Pope!"

He went on gazing at her till he felt dazzled, as if he were sitting in the sun. After a little time he said, "Well now, wife, what is there left to be now that you are Pope?"

She sat up very stiff and straight and said nothing.

He said again: "Well, wife, I hope you are contented at last with being Pope. There is nothing more you can be."

"We will see about that," she said. With that they both went to bed. She was as far as ever from being contented, and she could not get to sleep for thinking of what she should like to be next.

The fisherman, however, slept as fast as a top after his busy day. His wife tossed and turned from side to side the whole night through, thinking all the while what she could be next. But nothing would occur to her. When she saw the red dawn, she slipped off the bed and sat before the window to see the sun rise. As it came up she said: "Ah, I have it! Cannot I make the sun and moon to rise? Husband!" she cried and stuck her elbow in his ribs. "Wake up and go to your fish and tell him I want to be God."

The man was so fast asleep that when he started up he fell out of bed. He shook himself together, opened his eyes, and said, "Oh, wife, what did you say?"

"Husband," said she, "if I cannot get the power of making the sun and moon rise when I want them, I shall never have another quiet hour. Go to the fish and tell him so."

"Oh, wife!" said the man and fell on his knees to her. "The fish can really not do that for you. I grant you he could make you emperor and Pope. Do be contented with that, I beg of you."

She became wild with impatience and screamed out: "I can wait no longer. Go at once! I want to be God!"

Off he went as well as he could for fright. A dreadful storm arose, and he could hardly keep his feet. The houses and trees were blown down, and the mountains trembled, and rocks fell in the sea. The sky was quite black, and thunder and lightning was all around. The waves, crowned with foam, ran mountains high. Without being able to hear his own words he cried out:

O man, O man!—if man you be,
Or flounder, flounder, in the sea—
Such a tiresome wife I've got,
For she wants what I do not.

"Well, what now?" asked the flounder.

"Oh dear!" said the fisherman. "She wants to be God."

"Go home with you," said the flounder. "You will find her the way she was—in the old hovel."

And there they are sitting to this very day.

The Wishing Skin

(from *Old Hungarian Fairy Tales* collected by Baroness Orczy)

Once upon a time there lived a woodcutter in a little cottage at the foot of an old gigantic oak tree. He had a wife but no children, and together they lived humbly but very contentedly, for in front of his cottage he had a nice little garden in which he grew everything that was necessary for their daily food: fine wheat, with which to bake bread, and rich fruit and vegetables. He also had a cow that gave him an abundance of milk and sheep that yielded him soft wool, which his wife wove into garments for them.

One day a pedlar came wandering past the cottage with pots and pans and other goods for sale. The wife bought a thing or two from him that she needed, and he again went his way. When he had gone, the woodcutter found an old book of tales lying in the road that the pedlar had evidently dropped. He took it home to his wife, and in the evening when she sat at her spinning, he read some of the stories aloud to her. They were a curious lot of tales, all about fairies and magicians that granted people's wishes and changed woodcutters into kings.

That night the little woodcutter could not sleep a wink. He lay awake thinking of the fairies and picturing himself having one of those godmothers whose only duty seemed to be to wave her wand and fulfill requests. In the morning he went quite dejectedly to his work, quite different from his usual sprightly little self. He chopped the wood with a heavy heart for a time and finally threw down his ax in despair and sat down sullenly on the stump of a tree, wishing at least to see a fairy and persuade her to take an interest in him. His attention was presently attracted by a bright-eyed rabbit that seemed to have suddenly come from nowhere and that sat opposite him blinking one eye in a knowing way.

So absorbed was the little woodcutter in the castle he was building in the air that he never started, even when the rabbit suddenly began talking to him.

"Well, Mr. Woodcutter," said the rabbit, "and what can I do for you? You have been wishing to have a fairy godmother ever since last night. Now, though I am not your godmother, I know a thing or two. For instance, I know where the wishing skin lies, which the little fairies have been weaving for 300 years and which is now completed, and anyone wearing the same can have every wish fulfilled the moment he formulates it. Of course, as the skin is made of wishes, every time one is fulfilled it evaporates, and the skin becomes that much smaller. But then what does that matter? The little fairies have hidden the skin under a lightning-struck willow tree, but I have burrowed a hole and know exactly how to get at it. I will show it to you, if you like."

Thereupon the little rabbit darted off, and presently returned dragging a large bundle after it, which he spread out before the woodcutter's eager eyes.

"And is this skin really made of wishes?" asked the woodcutter. "Oh, Mr. Rabbit, please let me put it on just for a few minutes. I would like just to make one wish. I promise I will give it back to you directly."

The good-natured little rabbit willingly helped the woodcutter to put the magic skin on, which fit him somewhat tightly, but still it felt pretty comfortable.

"Oh! How I wish this skin were altogether mine," sighed the woodcutter, "and that I never need part with it."

Hardly had he uttered these words when he felt as if the skin fit him a shade tighter than before.

"Hallo!" said the rabbit, "what have you been wishing for? Certainly you seem to me to have diminished in size. Here, give me the skin. I must put it back where I found it, or the fairies will be after me."

But the woodcutter knew he need not give up his treasure anymore. So looking disdainfully at the rabbit he stalked off in the direction of his cottage, his head full of plans for future grandeur. But Mr. Bunny, in a great rage, lopped after him, yelling with all his might, till the woodcutter, losing all patience, turned round and screamed at him, "I wish you'd go to Jericho, and leave me alone."

When immediately the rabbit ran away as hard as he could tear, he felt the skin again tighten round him. He knew that Mr. Bunny had gone to Jericho and would trouble him no more.

When he got home, he told his wife his wonderful adventure, but she only thought he had been drinking, and advised him to go to bed and sleep it off, when, to convince her, he said, "I wish there were a fine supper table laid all ready here, with roast fowls, roast ducks, and roast turkeys, pies and puddings, and four flunkies to wait on my wife and me."

Hardly were the words out of his mouth when a most gorgeous table appeared in the center of the room. It was heavily laden with the most delicious dishes, fruits, and wines, while four servants in gold and silver livery stood waiting to serve the supper.

The wife could hardly believe her eyes, and they both sat down and ate and drank and made merry, for they felt that their future was likely to be a glorious one. Certainly, the little man felt himself a good bit smaller—his feet, when he sat, no longer reached the ground—but what of that? He would become so rich and proud that his stature would not be of the slightest consequence. So lifting a glass of wine high over his head, he said: "I wish to be a rich lord, with a castle instead of a cottage and lands and woods all my own. I wish to wear velvet garments and my wife to go about in nothing but silk dresses. I wish to eat off nothing but gold plates and to use glasses cut of pure diamonds. I wish...."

But his wife checked him just in time, for at every new wish he uttered he diminished 1 inch before her very eyes. And, lo! The humble cottage had disappeared, and they were sitting in a grand hall, with marble pillars and soft carpets. They looked out of the window, and though it was evening they could see distinctly a lovely garden planted with graceful trees and flowers, and there were fountains in crystal basins, while soft music filled the air.

The woodcutter looked at his wife and she at him. Poor little man, he was only 3 feet high then. But he was clad in a sumptuous coat and cloak of velvet lined with ermine. His wife was dressed in a lovely silk gown, with diamonds on her arms and neck. They could hardly contain themselves for joy, and the wife, seizing her little lord in her arms, began dancing round the room to the time of the distant music. The entrance of a number of lackies and maidservants asking his lordship for orders for the night reminded them of the duties of their new position. They marched off to their bedchamber in solemn state.

The next day they spent in visiting their extensive domains: the stables, coach houses, farms, and dairies. They found that they were indeed considered enormously wealthy—everybody bowed down to them and listened deferentially to all they had to say. The only thing that was very annoying was that the little lord felt that his 3 feet of stature were evidently a source of intense amusement to all his retainers and servants.

In the afternoon they ordered their gilded coach and six white horses to take them to pay calls on their neighbors, whom they hoped to dazzle with their great splendor. They set off in most gorgeous style, with an army of outriders and flunkies following the carriage. But to their intense astonishment the various neighboring lords had just as fine houses and gardens as their own and wore just as fine dresses and magnificent jewels as they did themselves. So they returned home in disgust. Joan especially was intensely annoyed. One lady on whom she called wore three more bracelets than she did. Another had seven more servants. And a third wore a dress embroidered with real pearls, while her own was only embroidered in silver. And one and all had sneered at her diminutive lord and had pointed to their own handsome husbands. She wished she could be richer and grander than they were so that they should be obliged to bow down before her, even at the cost of another foot off her husband's stature.

So after supper she talked to her lord about her grievances and pointed out to him that while he was merely the equal of his neighbors, they would always laugh at him. But once their superiors—say a royal duke or a prince—they would never dare to do so again. At first Jack refused to wish for anything else just yet. He felt himself quite small enough and did not think that any additional grandeur could compensate him for the loss of another 12 inches. However, at last his wife prevailed upon him, and just before going to bed he wished to become a royal duke, second only to the king and equal to any prince in the land.

The next morning Jack and Joan woke to find themselves in a royal palace with all the servants in royal liveries calling them their Royal Highnesses. All the lords and ladies in the land came to pay their respects to them as well. Joan was proud indeed. Not one lady wore such fine jewels or had such a number of servants and palaces as she had, and though her husband was now only 2 feet high, all the lords stood round him, loudly laughing at his jokes, and the ladies vied with one another as to who should lift him up into his chair. That very day the king himself was coming, with the queen and all his retinue, to pay a visit to the royal duke and duchess. Grand preparations were made for His Majesty's reception.

When the king and queen arrived, Jack and Joan received them in the grand hall of their palace. Poor little Jack! He felt very nervous when he had to kiss the Queen's hand because Joan had to lift him into a chair, which amused their majesties very much, and caused a titter among the other royal dukes, princes, and princesses. During the banquet, the diminutive royal duke had to sit on a very tall stool and had to have his food placed on his plate for him, as he could not reach the dishes. The King was quite convulsed with laughter, and hardly could eat anything. No one else dared to smile. But the Queen made sneering remarks to the duchess about her funny little husband.

That night Joan and Jack had a frightful difference of opinion. She wished to rule supreme over everybody so that even the King and the Queen, who had laughed at them, should have to come and do homage to her and her husband, whatever be his size. In fact, she wished to become the greatest empress in the world. Whereas Jack felt that another foot off his height would be a trial he could never undergo. However, his wife goaded him on till she had gained her point, and before the sun rose the next morning, the woodcutter and his wife became the most powerful emperor and empress in the world. There was not a king or a queen in the world that did not come to do homage before their imperial majesties. No war was declared between any nations or treaty signed without their consent. They exacted tribute from all duchies, principalities, and even kingdoms around. But alas! For the poor little emperor he was only 6 inches high and had to be carried in state on a cushion to all the great functions and to stand on a gold table when he received the ambassadors from foreign courts. At banquets and state dinners he had to sit on a little golden chair placed on the table, and be fed with a salt spoon out of the empress's plate.

Very soon he got tired of all this, more especially as, after a little while, Joan, now having reached the height of her ambition, took very little notice of him, she wouldn't allow him to have any voice in any of the affairs of state and grew tired of seeing her husband carried before her on a cushion. Finally she had a tiny doll's house built in the garden, into which she relegated her lord and master and only took him out to play with occasionally. Poor little Jack! He thought sorrowfully of the days when he was a fine grown man and cut wood in the forest and was master of his own little home by the old oak tree. He cursed the rabbit, the fairies, the pedlar, and chiefly his own blind stupidity in wishing to change his own contented happy lot for all this gilded misery.

At last one day, looking out of one of the tiny windows of his doll's house, he saw a woodcutter going along merrily with his bundle of fagots, whistling a lively tune. The poor little emperor took his jeweled crown, which he always wore, off his head, and throwing it violently on the ground, so that the gems were scattered in all directions, he said—"Oh, how I wish I were a full-grown man, a woodcutter again, with my wife in my own little cottage, not dreaming even of such things as kings and emperors."

When he had spoken, in one moment, the magnificent palace, the exquisite gardens had vanished, and he sat in his big armchair opposite his wife who was knitting, his feet touched the ground, and his arm reached to where Joan was sitting. They fell into each other's arms. Was it all a dream, little readers? I cannot tell you, but all I know is that henceforth Jack and Joan lived humbly in their little cottage contented and happy ever after.

(Reprinted by permission of the publisher.)

Joseph and His Brothers

(from Genesis 37-50)

Jacob, renamed Israel by God, had many children by several wives, and he loved Joseph more than all his children because he was the son of his old age. Jacob made Joseph a coat of many colors. When Joseph's brothers saw that their father loved him more than all the others, they hated him and were hateful to him.

Joseph had a dream that he told to his brothers. In his dream he saw that they were binding sheaves in the field, and Joseph's sheaves arose and stood upright. The sheaves of the brothers stood around and made obeisance to Joseph's. The brothers asked Joseph if he was indeed to reign over them and have dominion over them. This made them hate Joseph all the more.

Joseph dreamed yet another dream in which he saw that the sun and the moon and the 11 stars made obeisance to him. Joseph told his father and brothers this dream. Again the brothers became envious of him.

The brothers were out with their flocks for an extended time, and Jacob sent Joseph to check on his brothers and their animals and to report to him. When Joseph's brothers saw him coming, they conspired to kill him. The brothers argued, but when Joseph came to where they were, they stripped him of his coat of many colors. They then took him and cast him into an empty pit. They sat down to eat, and one of the brothers, Judah, told his brothers that they should sell Joseph to the Ishmaelites instead of killing him. And so they sold Joseph into slavery. They received 20 pieces of silver for Joseph who was then taken to Egypt.

The brothers killed a goat and dipped the coat of many colors in its blood. They took the coat to their father and told him they had found it. Of course, Jacob recognized the coat and concluded that Joseph had been torn apart by a wild beast. Jacob mourned for his son for many days, and his children were not able to comfort him in his grief.

Joseph was sold again to an officer of the Egyptian pharaoh's who was the captain of the guard. Joseph served as the overseer of the captain's house and became a prosperous man. Everything that Joseph touched seemed to be blessed. The captain's wife tried to tempt Joseph, who refused her advances. She caught him by his clothing, and when he escaped her, she held onto it. She showed her husband the piece of clothing and accused Joseph of making advances to her.

Joseph was put into a prison, and even there Joseph was recognized as being special. The keeper of the prison took mercy on Joseph and put him in charge of all the other prisoners. The pharaoh's butler and baker had angered him, so the pharaoh had them put into the same prison as Joseph. Each of them had dreams that Joseph interpreted for them. The butler would be restored to service with the pharaoh in three days, according to Joseph. Joseph interpreted the baker's dream as well, and foretold that within three days the pharaoh would have him hung from a tree. Both of these predictions came true.

Two years later the pharaoh had two dreams that troubled him. The butler remembered Joseph's dream interpretations and told the pharaoh of him. The pharaoh sent for Joseph. Joseph told him that God had showed the pharaoh what was about to happen through his dreams. He predicted that there would be seven good years of plenty, seven poor ones, and seven years of famine. The pharaoh ordered his men to gather food during the seven years of plenty to store and keep for the seven years of famine. Joseph impressed the pharaoh and therefore was placed over all the people, only second to the pharaoh. Joseph was treated as royalty. Everything came to pass, and the Egyptians survived the famine.

People from other countries also suffering from the famine came to Egypt asking to buy food. Joseph's 10 brothers went to Egypt to buy corn. Joseph recognized his brothers, but they did not recognize him. Jacob had kept his youngest son, Benjamin, at home to keep him safe from danger, not wanting to possibly lose all his sons. Joseph demanded that the 10 brothers bring their other brother to him. He told them that they must go, and one of them would stay in prison until the youngest brother was brought to him. Joseph sent food and money back with the brothers. Jacob refused to let them return with Benjamin.

When all the food they had brought back was gone, Jacob again sent his sons out to buy food. He agreed that Benjamin must go with them this time, and they would take gifts to this man in Egypt. When the brothers returned to Egypt, Joseph saw that Benjamin was among them, and he prepared a feast. As he had done before, Joseph ordered his men to provide corn for the brothers and to again put their money in the sacks too. Additionally, Joseph told his men to put his silver cup in the sack of Benjamin.

Early the next morning the brothers prepared to go home. Joseph had men overtake them and accuse them of doing evil to him. They were returned to Joseph and he told them that the man who had stolen his cup would become his servant. When the cup was found in Benjamin's sack, they pleaded with Joseph, telling him that their father was an old man and that he would die if Benjamin did not return.

Joseph cried and revealed to them that he was Joseph, their brother, whom they had sold into slavery. Joseph felt that this had happened so that he would be able to save his family when the famine struck everywhere. With this, he told them to bring their father to him. The pharaoh welcomed Jacob, known by God as Israel, and his family to Egypt. The 12 sons became the heads of the 12 tribes of Israel.

Discussion

This story from the Bible and "The Singing Bone" are excellent for promoting discussion about siblings. Why were Joseph's brothers jealous of him? How did Joseph handle the situation when his brothers sold him into slavery? Was he vengeful and eager to get revenge on them? Why was the older brother jealous in "The Singing Bone"? Do you think the older brother believed he'd gotten away with the murder? This could then be generalized to a discussion about times we have been jealous or envious of our brothers or sisters.

The fear of having a new baby sibling was last on the list of what children feared, but on the other hand, adults felt it would be among the most stressful fears of children. Other fears children had involving the family included fighting by parents. This fear ranked much higher on the list by children. Because family structures today include the reality of divorce and stepfamilies, children are experiencing more stress than just that that is related to the birth of a new brother or sister. With this in mind, the bibliography includes a variety of family situations and possibilities.

Activities

- Ask the children with brothers or sisters to share about good times they have with their brothers and sisters.

- Ask them to share some of the problems they have with brothers or sisters.

- Encourage the children to consider whether the good times outweigh the problems. Brainstorm ways to solve the problems.

- Have those with siblings brainstorm about the positive and negative experiences they might have if they were "only" children.

- Have the children brainstorm about whether it would be harder or easier for parents if they had only one child. Is it harder or easier for the children to have siblings?

- Ask the children to interview older relatives to find out their opinions on having brothers or sisters. Now that they are grown-up, did their opinions change with age? If so, why?

- Children can read stories and books and observe how families are described in them. They can compare and contrast their observations.

Bibliography

Banks, Ann. *When Your Parents Get a Divorce, a Kid's Journal.* Illustrations by Cathy Bobak. New York: Puffin Books, 1990.
   Knowing that divorce is difficult, the author has written some constructive activities and leaves plenty of space for writing so that children may work through their feelings. There is a special tear-out parent's guide that includes strategies and suggestions to make things easier for the whole family.

Baum, Louis. *After Dark.* Illustrations by Susan Varley. New York: Overlook Press, 1990.
   Although it is time for bed, a small girl will not go to sleep until her mother returns from late-night shopping.

Berenstain, Stan, and Jan Berenstain. *The Berenstain Bears Are a Family.* New York: Random House, 1991.
   All the Bear family relations—parents, siblings, grandparents, aunts, uncles, and cousins—show up in this book that is about what a family means.

Bloom, Suzanne. *A Family for Jamie.* New York: Clarkson N. Potter, 1991.
   Although Dan and Molly can make cookies and birdhouses, they cannot make a baby, so they adopt Jamie and share with him their life and love.

Blume, Judy. *The One in the Middle Is the Green Kangaroo.* Illustrations by Irene Trivas. New York: Bradbury Press, 1991.
   Freddy hates being the middle one in the family until he gets a part in the school play.

_____. *The Pain and the Great One.* New York: Bradbury Press, 1984.
   A sister and her little brother take turns telling their side of the same story. The viewpoints from each vividly demonstrate sibling differences.

Clifford, Eth. *The Remembering Box*. Boston: Houghton Mifflin, 1985.

Nine-year-old Joshua's weekly visits to his beloved grandmother on the Jewish Sabbath give him an understanding of love, family, and tradition, which helps him accept her death.

dePaola, Tomie. *Now One Foot, Now the Other*. New York: Putnam, 1981.

When his grandfather suffers a stroke, Bobby teaches him to walk, just as his grandfather once taught him.

Hines, Anna Grossnickle. *Jackie's Lunch Box*. New York: Greenwillow, 1991.

It is hard for Jackie when her sister, Carla, goes off to school, so Jackie spends her time planning on how to greet Carla when she comes home from school.

Hoberman, Mary Ann. *Fathers, Mothers, Sisters, Brothers*. Illustrations by Marylin Hafner. Boston: Joy Street Books, 1991.

Humorous and serious poems celebrate every kind of family member, including aunts, uncles, stepbrothers, sisters, cousins, and even cats.

Johnson, Dolores. *What Will Mommy Do When I'm at School?* New York: Macmillan, 1990.

A child worries about how her mother will cope at home on her own while she is at school.

Keats, Ezra Jack. *Peter's Chair*. New York: Harper & Row, 1967.

The classic book about an older brother's distress when the family paints his old things pink for the new baby. He runs away from home and grows up in the process.

Livingston, Myra Cohn. *Poems for Brothers, Poems for Sisters*. Illustrations by Jean Zallinger. New York: Holiday House, 1991.

A collection of poems exploring the relationship between brothers and sisters.

Munsch, Robert. *Good Families Don't*. Illustrations by Alan Daniel. New York: Dell, 1990.

An outrageous, humorous look at what good families do or do not do.

Peterson, Jeanne Whitehouse. *I Have a Sister, My Sister Is Deaf*. Illustrations by Deborah Kogan Ray. New York: Harper & Row, 1977.

A young girl describes how her deaf sister experiences everyday things.

Rosenberg, Maxine B. *Talking About Stepfamilies.* New York: Bradbury Press, 1990.
Children and adults who have become part of stepfamilies describe their experiences in coping with new stepparents and stepsiblings.

Sendak, Maurice. *Pierre, a Cautionary Tale in Five Chapters and a Prologue.* New York: Harper & Row, 1962.
A classic story told in verse of the problems of Pierre and his parents.

Smith, Wendy. *The Lonely, Only Mouse.* New York: Puffin Books, 1988.
What an introduction to family life! Thelonius is an only mouse who is lonely until his cousin Charlie, who is one of 26 children, comes to stay, making things look very different.

Viorst, Judith. *Alexander and the Terrible, Horrible, No Good, Very Bad Day.* Illustrations by Ray Cruz. New York: Atheneum, 1973.
Have you ever had a day when everything went wrong that could? Of course, you have. We all have. This is Alexander's story, and his brothers do not make it any easier for him.

_____. *Alexander, Who Used to Be Rich Last Sunday.* Illustrations by Ray Cruz. New York: Atheneum, 1978.
Alexander and his money are quickly parted, yet he realizes that there are many things a dollar can do. His brothers are part of his poverty.

Walter, Mildred Pitts. *My Mama Needs Me.* Illustrations by Pat Cummings. New York: Lothrop, Lee & Shepard, 1983.
Jason wants to help but is not sure that his mother needs him at all after she brings home a new baby from the hospital.

_____. *Two and Too Much.* Illustrations by Pat Cummings. New York: Bradbury Press, 1990.
Seven-year-old Brandon's attempt to take care of his two-year-old sister, Gina, results in one disaster after another.

Widerberg, Siv. *The Big Sister.* Illustrations by Cecilia Torudd. New York: R & S Books (distributed by Farrar, Straus and Giroux), 1989.
The older sister was always biggest, oldest, tallest, and strongest and knew better than anyone that little sisters do not know anything at all. But there was one thing the older sister could never be, and sometimes that was what she wanted to be most of all.

Williams, Suzanne. *Mommy Doesn't Know My Name.* Illustrations by
   Andrew Shachat. Boston: Houghton Mifflin, 1990.
   Mommy calls Hannah all sorts of names except her own, leaving
Hannah to wonder if Mommy really does know who she is.

Ziefert, Harriet. *Getting Ready for New Baby.* Illustrations by Laura Rader.
   New York: HarperCollins, 1990.
   Insightful, compassionate questions and answers for preschoolers
when a new baby is on the way. It explains the physical and emotional facts
of life.

Index

About the Author

Norma J. Livo received her bachelor's, master's and doctorate degrees from the University of Pittsburgh. She was employed as a geophysical assistant with Gulf Research Laboratory, as a demonstration teacher at the Falk Laboratory School with the University of Pittsburgh, and as professor at the University of Colorado at Denver.

She has coauthored *Storytelling: Process and Practice, Storytelling Activities, Folk Stories of the Hmong, Storytelling Folklore Sourcebook*, and *Who's Endangered on Noah's Ark?*, all published by Libraries Unlimited. Other books include *Joining In* with Yellow Moon Press, *Free Rein* with Allyn Bacon, and *Hmong Textile Design* with Stemmer House.

She is a columnist for the *Rocky Mountain News* and serves on the board of directors for the National Association for the Preservation and Perpetuation of Storytelling. Norma was also president of the Colorado Council of the International Reading Association and organizer of the Rocky Mountain Storytelling Conference.

She and her husband, George, are the parents of four fantastic young folks and the grandparents of seven grandchildren.